IMAGES
of America

LOST AMUSEMENT PARKS
OF SOUTHERN CALIFORNIA
THE POSTWAR YEARS

D1572410

BUBBLES THE PILOT WHALE. Two sailors—one untraditionally attired in short shorts and flirty black pumps—stand atop a diving board to feed an enthusiastically breaching whale at Marineland of the Pacific, which opened in 1954 and was located in Rancho Palos Verdes. (Courtesy of the George Mann Archives.)

ON THE COVER: MIDCENTURY MODERN SEASIDE PARK. The Ocean Skyway at Pacific Ocean Park in Santa Monica allowed riders a bird's-eye view of the amusement park, beach, and ocean waves from the safety of a clear, futuristic bubble. (Courtesy of Bison Archives.)

IMAGES
of America

LOST AMUSEMENT PARKS
OF SOUTHERN CALIFORNIA
THE POSTWAR YEARS

Lisa Hallett Taylor

ARCADIA
PUBLISHING

Published by Arcadia Publishing
Charleston, South Carolina

Printed in the United States of America

Library of Congress Control Number: 2021940506

For all general information, please contact Arcadia Publishing:
Telephone 843-853-2070
Fax 843-853-0044
E-mail sales@arcadiapublishing.com
For customer service and orders:
Toll-Free 1-888-313-2665

Visit us on the Internet at www.arcadiapublishing.com

*For the child whose face lights up with each rotation
of the carousel: may you always find that special
someone who waves back, even if it's a memory*

CONTENTS

FOREWORD

You are holding in your hands what is probably the best history of Southern California amusement parks—from kiddie parks, like the ones Walt Disney visited with his girls and was inspired by, to pleasure piers and roadside attractions to theme parks.

That's where I come in. I had the good fortune and privilege to work for the man who I believe was responsible for creating the industry that became known as "theme parks." That man was Walt Disney. I began my career in animation at the Disney studio in 1952. I had been drawing since I was two years old (as documented by my mom). After seeing my first Disney animated cartoon, I knew that's what I wanted to do. It was while working as an assistant animator that we had our first glimpse of the project Walt was developing. We had heard rumors, but when we saw Walt dressed like a cowboy, riding a stagecoach on the studio lot, we knew something big was in the works. That something became Disneyland.

The model shop, which later became known as WED, was where all the magic happened. I used to hang out there and loved seeing the creative work being done. I soon realized that's what I wanted to do. I had outgrown animation and wanted to be a designer.

In 1959, Walt invited me to join WED. He didn't know me, but he had seen my exhibit in the studio library that included a series of propellers in bottles and was intrigued by them. That was Walt's first introduction to Roland "Rolly" Crump, and for me, a dream came true. Working at WED was a ride in itself. So much happening at the same time. All being designed and built by a handful of artists, Walt would later name us *Imagineers*. We were creating things we had never done before, and we were learning as we went along.

During the next decade, I had the great joy of being involved in the development of some of the most popular attractions at Disneyland. One of my first assignments was It's a Small World for the New York World's Fair in 1964. Remembering my propeller exhibit at the studio, Walt asked me to design the marquee for the ride. He envisioned it as a tower of propellers [like a giant mobile], also known as the Tower of the Four Winds.

The Enchanted Tiki Room was where I learned the importance of research for any new project and is where I learned to sculpt for the first time. Maybe my favorite assignment was bringing It's a Small World from New York to Disneyland and designing the facade and clock for the entrance to the ride while paying tribute to and being true to the style of Mary Blair [who created color schemes and character designs]. And, of course, there's The Haunted Mansion. My main contribution was the Museum of the Weird, based on a series of sketches I did that would have become an extension of the museum had Walt not passed away when he did.

After leaving Disney in the 1970s and starting my own design company, I took what I learned and brought that incredible experience to the new projects I was asked to design. One, in particular, was the dark ride Knott's Bear-y Tales. I was able to incorporate some design elements I hadn't been able to use before, including magic, mixed lighting effects, and awakening the visitors' senses of smell by enjoying the aroma of pies baking.

A question I'm frequently asked is, "Why, after all this time, is Disneyland still loved and enjoyed by so many?" My answer is there are several reasons. The atmosphere represents the different styles and strengths of the various artists who created the attractions. The park is charming; it hugs you. From the time you enter, you feel you have come home. Either a home you remember or one you wish you knew. It reflects the man, the memories, and the imagination of the person who dreamed it.

I have a metaphor I like to use: Disneyland is like a huge, incredible salad filled with so many wonderful ingredients—something for everyone. It's put together with meticulous attention to detail. It leaves other parks seemingly . . . just basic lettuce and tomato.

—Roland "Rolly" Crump

ACKNOWLEDGEMENTS

My sincere thanks to the many individuals and families who shared wonderful images of themselves, their families, and ancestors captured in moments of happiness at long-gone parks or on rides.

Thanks to Rolly Crump for a lovely foreword and for helping to create It's a Small World, a ride that exceeded my anticipation and always leaves me feeling enchanted.

To the Venice Heritage Foundation for their help and suggestions when nearly everything was closed during the first waves of the pandemic.

To Mary Susa and the Irvine Historical Society for sharing their Lion Country Safari and Newport Harbor Buffalo Ranch archives.

To my editor, Angel Prohaska, for her patience and persistence.

To Marc Wanamaker for his guidance and expertise.

To David Starkman and Susan Pinsky for their generosity and education in 3-D photography.

To Sharon Marie, daughter of Carolina Cotton, for keeping her mother's awesome cowgirl spirit alive.

To Candace English for the delightful photographs and stories of her grandparents' Tiny Town in Compton.

To Russ Keller for sharing his fascinating archives—I enjoyed the trip up to the mountains.

To Robin Stewart Hall for his generosity and expertise in amusement park design.

To Alan Hess for his knowledge and insight into Modernism and Midcentury park architecture.

To Harvey Jordan for sharing his divine Bible Storyland collection.

To J. Eric Lynxwiler for his Knott's Berry Farm expertise and kind responses.

To Steve Oftelie and Chris Jepsen of the Orange County Archives for their knowledge, time, and willingness to dive deep into regional history.

To my brother, Bruce, and the Blattners for sharing some of these early adventures with me.

To my children, James and Chloe, for letting me show and experience rides and parks with them and helping me see things through their eyes.

To Thom for his love and roll-up-his-sleeves help and support; for always being there.

To Robert and Dolores for moving to Southern California and being such loving parents.

To anyone I haven't mentioned, thank you so much for taking the time to help, research, and share great stories.

IMAGE COURTESY KEY

BA	Bison Archives
OCA	Orange County Archives
HC/OCA	Hurlbut Collection, Orange County Archives
BF	The Biren family
JBH	The family of James Barry Herron, photographer
SFA	The Starkman family archives, photographs by architect Maxwell Starkman
GMA	The George Mann Archives
NDF	The Nick DeWolf Foundation
RKC	Russ Keller collection, the Rim of the World Historical Society
UWWBC	University of Wyoming, American Heritage Center, William Boyd Papers
UCIHM	Hugh R. McMillan photograph MS.R.035, Special Collections & Archives, University of California (UC), Irvine Libraries
UCIWG	Wally Gerhardt photograph MS.R.023, Special Collections & Archives, University of California (UC), Irvine Libraries
RSH	Robin Stewart Hall, amusement park designer
CCE	Sharon Marie, Carolina Cotton Estate
CTL	Conejo Through the Lens, Thousand Oaks Library
CTL/HN	Conejo Through the Lens, CTLnos027, CTLnos108, Herb Noseworthy photographs
CTL/MJR	Conejo Through the Lens, CTLrob064, Mary Jo Robertson photograph
CTL/DB	Conejo Through the Lens, CTLbir01, David Birenbaum
UCLA	*Los Angeles Times* Photographic Archive, Library Special Collections, Charles E. Young Research Library, University of California, Los Angeles.
TTP	Candace English, Tiny Town Park
MVCHCC	Jeff Price and the City of Mission Viejo, California Heritage Committee Collection
WF	Wendi Fletcher
RH	Robert Hermann
RWH	Robert W. Hermann
JC	Jess Corey
HBC	Herbert Bruce Cross
BBHJ	Bruce Bushman, artist, Harvey Jordan collection

If not noted after the caption, the image is courtesy of the author.

INTRODUCTION

What if a favorite amusement park closed—as many did during the pandemic lockdown—but never reopened? Imagine the feeling of never again being able to walk through a favorite place, to explore old rides and experiences inside its gates that have become so much more familiar and meaningful with each visit? Or to never climb on board the miniature train or to ride a favorite zebra on the carousel that has been there since forever, it seems.

That's what it feels like when something is lost and gone forever. That place is physically gone; all that remains are memories, photographs, stories, and some home videos.

But they were here, these amusement parks and roadside attractions, in full force. At one time, Southern California could claim it was the family vacation and tourist capital of the world, with its beaches, mountains, deserts, all that sunshine, and amusement parks. There were so many amusement and theme parks that nobody could visit them all, from San Diego to Santa Barbara and every burg in between. There were so many, it's unlikely that anyone could have been aware of them all. In the most populous region of the most populous state, hundreds of cities tend to erase remnants of the past to modernize and accommodate more residents.

After World War II, Southern California was inundated with people moving to the region, companies building headquarters or factories, and developers sizing up all of that land being used to grow things like grapefruit, celery, and lima beans. Tract houses were built, all looking the same from an aerial view, but people were proud to have their own homes and start families. Infrastructure was created: roads, highways, commercial buildings, power, and sewage to provide for and facilitate the lives and needs of growing communities.

Still, people wanted to have fun again, to experience that spontaneous pleasure they missed during the war years; something simple, like going with family or friends to a pleasure pier, enjoying the warmth of the sand, followed by arcade games, hot dogs, and rides on the Ferris wheel. These casual outings didn't cost much, nor did they require advance planning or reservations. "Kiddielands" were built throughout Los Angeles and the San Fernando Valley—where the new homes and communities were sprouting. Admission was inexpensive, and the rides were targeted to children under age 10. Located near shopping centers or major intersections, they did a decent business for a while. And the young baby boomers loved them.

But two decades into the postwar period, Southern California's seaside parks were languishing or worse. That perfect setting and scenario of a beach, a boardwalk, a midway, thrilling rides, hamburgers, and weird things to see were pretty much a thing of the recent past. "The Nu-Pike will last a couple more years, but its death was foreordained in the 1950s when Walt Disney opened Disneyland," wrote columnist Bob Wells in a 1968 *Long Beach Press-Telegram* article. "Tomorrowland replaced the snake lady and the geek, the Matterhorn replaced the Cyclone Racer, and Tinker Bell replaced the girlie shows."

Walt Disney is said to have had a childlike sense of fun and curiosity. He was a boots-on-the-ground researcher who visited local kiddielands and parks with his family, studying people and their behaviors. His position and wealth allowed him to travel to some of the world's finest amusement parks to analyze their successes. At Tivoli Gardens in Copenhagen, Disney noted a magical place in which the landscaping was designed as part of the whole park environment, disguising equipment so that visitors could focus on the splendor. Tivoli was also meticulously cleaned and maintained.

Out of this research and development, Disneyland was born in 1955. Amusement parks in Southern California—and the rest of the world—have never been the same.

Other parks tried either to compete directly or to find a theme. There were parks with land animals, marine animals, birds, and beer. Top Midcentury Modernist architects designed a few of Southern California's amusement parks and attractions, but most people weren't there for the aesthetics. Entrepreneurs tried to recreate every type of celebrity in wax, from old movie stars to Joan of Arc. Parks focused on automobiles or interpretations of different cultures. Every other amusement park had or was the "world's greatest" or "world's biggest." And if that didn't bring people in, then surely a chimp would always prove irresistible, especially if it danced or smoked a cigar.

Reasons vary for an amusement park to close: competition from other parks, safety and maintenance costs, economic or financial issues, or just changing tastes. "While many pier parks are remembered fondly, the sea is terrible for maintenance," explained Robin Stewart Hall, who was a designer and master planner of Magic Mountain and Knott's Berry Farm and has used his skills at parks throughout the world. "The track record for ride safety hasn't been that great. In the beginning, this was a holdover from the traveling carnivals, and things got lots of wear and tear with the constant setup and tear down. It also takes a lot of capital to train staff and maintain, which isn't showy, so it can be last in line to get funding. The government was very slow to set standards, and sadly, many owners were in it just for the money. Parks are also like small cities in that they need knowledgeable operators or the operations go downhill fast. It's tough to get people to come back with one bad experience."

Look at what was once considered entertainment in Southern California. Who's ready to go spend a day on the dusty streets of Corriganville or ride the Banana Train at Pacific Ocean Park? Or does the region have a short memory, with places needing to be changed or reinvented every decade?

"Southern California's cycle is shorter because there is so much competition," said Hall. "In smaller markets where a park might be the only game in town, the locals tend to become loyal to their branded park. The LA market for parks is thought of as an arms race. Planning, along with attraction mix, is considered top secret, as it can mean a successful year or a disaster."

This is not a lament for what once was, but rather an exploration of the recent past. Many people remember long-gone parks, and for others, it's an opportunity to discover a world that can only be imagined.

One

KIDDIELANDS

After World War II, many returning GIs married, eventually finding jobs in California's aerospace, manufacturing, or other industries. Some started families and bought low-down or no-down-payment tract homes in the suburbs. Beginning in the mid-1940s, children's amusement parks were suddenly everywhere, enjoying a heyday in the 1950s to mid-1960s and continuing in some places through the 1970s. Kiddieland was not a franchise; it was a universal term for a children's amusement park with pint-sized rides for children mostly under age 10. These child-centric parks were permanent and familiar yet still able to evoke thrills. The rides were fairly standard: a train, carousel, cars, rockets, planes, trolleys, ponies, and a Ferris wheel. Many children thrive on predictability and would delight in choosing their favorite car or pony each time they visited.

Kiddielands were strategically located near shopping centers or restaurants and on main thoroughfares that could be viewed by children from the backseats of their parents' Chevys. A churning Ferris wheel and a whiff of sweaty ponies were the best advertising for new and repeating customers. As suburbs developed, property taxes and insurance liabilities were increased, and the land became more valuable; grocery chains or apartment complexes became more profitable than penny-ride amusement parks.

Heavily populated Los Angeles County boasted the most kiddie parks. Among them were the aptly named Kiddielands in Redondo Beach, Westchester, Woodland Hills, and West Los Angeles. There was also Collins Kiddieland in Studio City, Uncle Ben's Kiddyland in North Hollywood and Panorama City, Billy Puffer's on Laurel Canyon Boulevard, Rockwell in Hawthorne, Lucas in Silver Lake, Lombardi in Topanga Canyon, Hitching Post in Panorama City, Victor's on Venice Boulevard, Tiny Town in Compton, Tinkertown in Leimert Park, Uncle Blaine's in Inglewood, Streamline Park in Pico Rivera, and Clock Kiddieland in Norwalk.

Other Southland parks included a Garden Square Kiddieland in Garden Grove, the Little Colonel's Auction Village in Baldwin Park, Crawford's Corner in El Monte, Humpty Dumpty Land in La Puente, Lil-Dude in Lancaster, Duke Jones near Ojai, Perris Hill Kiddieland, and Playland in San Bernardino. Among San Diego County's parks were Wagon Wheel, Happy Hollow, and Marshal Scotty's Playland.

A frequent weekend visitor to Beverly Park, the Griffith Park carousel, and Crawford's Corner was Walt Disney, who would bring his daughters and closely observe the rides and people's reactions to them. It took years of research and development before he knew what he wanted and where he wanted to build it.

BEVERLY PARK, C. 1947. Actor Dan Duryea, star of Westerns and film noirs, treats sons Richard and Pete to an afternoon of kid-sized thrills. The park was in operation from about 1945 to 1974 and was probably the most centrally located kiddieland in Los Angeles. (BA.)

KID-SIZED RIDES FOR THE BABY BOOMERS. Rides at Beverly Park included a Little Dipper roller coaster, boats, a Streamliner train, Dodgem bumper cars, a pony cart track, a carousel, cars, and a haunted castle. Next door was Beverly Ponyland. (BA.)

LAP BARS CONTROLLED THE HEIGHT. Tiny Wendi Fletcher and her grandmother, Helen Rush, take a whirl on Beverly Park's helicopter ride during a visit in 1960. Rides were modified, sold, and added throughout the park's 30-year existence. (WF.)

THRILLS IN BEVERLY HILLS ADJACENT. Puffy-sleeved Deborah Kalantari leans back in bliss while riding Bulgy the Whale at Beverly Park, which was within walking distance of her house. The much-loved park entertained locals and children of Hollywood stars at the corner of La Cienega and Beverly Boulevards. (Deborah Kalantari.)

COASTER, BUILT IN 1946. Sam Biren captured another man photographing Beverly Park's Little Dipper as their children rode the small-scale track. The 12-person steel roller coaster eventually made its way to Magic Mountain as the Magic Flyer and Goliath Jr. (BF.)

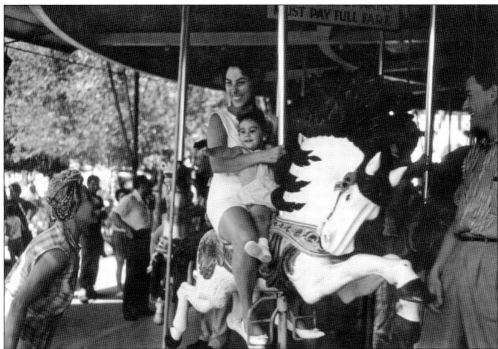

C.W. PARKER CAROUSEL. Helen Rush looks on as her granddaughter, Wendi, and her daughter, Sharon, ride the prettiest horse at Beverly Park. Operator Dave Bradley bought the 1916-built carousel in 1947; it was previously at nearby Ocean Park and Santa Monica piers. Bradley & Kaye refurbished, recreated, and sold carousel animals to other parks. (WF.)

Movie Star Sighting. Actress Lana Turner and her daughter, Cheryl, enjoy a day at Beverly Park in 1947. Many celebrities and their families visited the park throughout the years, including Carol Burnett, Errol Flynn, and Janet Leigh with her daughter Jamie Lee Curtis. (BA.)

David Bradley, Owner. In 1945, Dave Bradley and Don Kaye bought the kiddie park. Kaye returned to the music industry, but Bradley kept the Bradley & Kaye name for his amusement manufacturing company. Walt Disney was a frequent park visitor who discussed the business with Bradley. (BA.)

ANTIQUE CIRCUS WAGON. Wendi Fletcher and her grandfather, Morris Rush, take a horse and cart through Beverly Park's Western town. Bradley decorated the park with vintage circus wagons that he later sold to film studios. (WF.)

CHOO-CHOO WITH A VIEW. Jordan Biren and his mother, Pat, enjoy a ride on the train. Before Bradley became proprietor, Beverly Park was known as Tinker Town in the early 1940s. Besides Beverly Park, locals referred to it as "Tinker Town," "Kiddieland," or "Pony Land" (for the pony stables next door). (BF.)

THE BUSINESS OF BIRTHDAYS. Many recall the fabulous and frequent (scheduled every 15 minutes) birthday parties at Beverly Park. Included in a party package were tickets, balloons, a clown cake, favors, and refreshments. (BF.)

TOO MANY CHOICES? Abe Birenzweig has his hands full with his five grandchildren at Beverly Park around 1955. The park was a popular and convenient place for grandparents, parents, and, starting in the late 1960s, divorced dads to entertain the kids on weekends. (BF.)

END OF THE LINE, 1970s. A little girl delights in her power of riding a mini-motorcycle at one of Beverly Park's newer rides. A lease hike and competition from larger parks forced Bradley to close the park in 1974, making way for the multilevel Beverly Center shopping and restaurant complex. (BA.)

WENDELL "BUD" HURLBUT. The designer, fabricator, and engineer was a mover and shaker in midcentury amusement rides and parks of the region. Hurlbut had his own amusement company in Whittier and later, Buena Park, and built rides for many local parks, starting with kiddielands in the 1940s. (HC/OCA.)

AMUSEMENT PARK IN EL MONTE, C. 1947. One of Hurlbut's earliest ventures was the kiddieland at Crawford's Five Points, a popular market and shopping center. Crawford's threw holiday parties, was profiled by *Life* magazine, and held contests and giveaways of beans, watermelon, and slices of the world's biggest cheese (12,000 pounds). (HC/OCA.)

A HURLBUT STEAM ENGINE. Bud Hurlbut was a miniature train enthusiast and builder who loved seeing his locomotives at kiddie parks and in private collections. The mechanical genius is credited with convincing family friend Walter Knott to add rides to his Berry Stand for patrons waiting in line at Mrs. Knott's Chicken Dinner Restaurant in Buena Park. (HC/OCA.)

An Explosion of Postwar Parks. In the mid-1940s, people were ready to forget the pains of the war for a few hours and celebrate at amusement parks like the one Hurlbut designed at Crawford's

Corner in El Monte. Rides included a train, Ferris wheel, cars, boats, and a carousel. (HC/OCA.)

GLEAMING KIDDIE CARS, CRAWFORD'S. In addition to Hurlbut Amusement Co. of Whittier, some of the top manufacturers' names in kiddie rides included H.E. Ewart of Compton, J.L. Lucas of Los Angeles, and Eyerly Aircraft of Salem, Oregon. A shortage of materials like steel, carried over from the war, challenged manufacturers to find alternatives. (HC/OCA.)

BILLY PUFFER TRAIN, 1946. Before opening Tiny Town in Compton, Harry "Matt" Matthews built a scale model of a Union Pacific train in which he and his wife, Beatrice, took their grandchildren and neighborhood kids for rides. Bud Hurlbut built the 32-passenger Billy Puffer train. (TTP.)

WELCOME TO TINY TOWN, C. 1944. After building more kiddie rides, Tiny Town found a permanent home at Long Beach Boulevard and Olive Street (now Alondra Boulevard). Matt and Beatrice opened Tiny Town Park in Compton and enjoyed more than a dozen years of success, thanks to the couple's hard work, civic-mindedness, and Matt's knack for public relations. (TTP.)

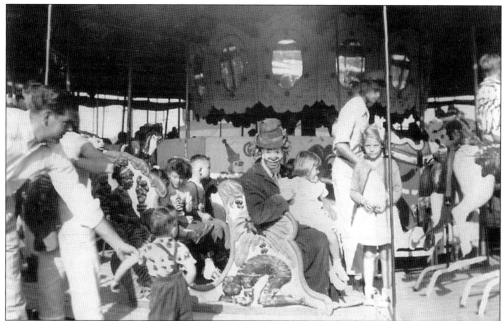

NUTSY THE CLOWN, 1951. Nutsy starred in a local daily television show and was a frequent guest at Tiny Town. Matt Matthews's Hollywood connections meant the park was visited by Southland kiddie-TV favorites like Russ Clark (Uncle Archie), along with Stan Freberg and Cecil the Sea Serpent. (TTP.)

TINKER TOWN IN LEIMERT PARK. In a 1948 *Billboard* article, Bob Austin is credited with creating one of Los Angeles's first kiddie parks. The entrepreneur modified Jeeps and Mack trucks into double-deck buses, trains, and a mobile movie theater. Besides his Crenshaw Boulevard location, Austin brought Tinker Town to weekend fairs and civic events throughout the Southland in the 1940s–1960s. (HC/OCA.)

CELEBRITY ENDORSEMENTS. Local TV and movie cowboy Doye O'Dell's name appeared briefly above the Lucas Kiddieland sign in Silver Lake. The park made news in 1951 when Shetland ponies busted a fence and headed up Riverside Drive to munch on greener pastures. Police corralled the ponies and returned them back to Lucas. (HC/OCA.)

ANOTHER HURLBUT RAILROAD. Uncle Ben's Kiddyland had at least two locations: North Hollywood and Panorama City. In 1956, actor/activist Phil Ahn treated 25 South Korean war orphans to a day at Uncle Ben's Panorama City park. Ahn owned nearby Moongate Restaurant and costarred with the kids in the film *Battle Hymn*. (HC/OCA.)

Uncle Ben's Sepulveda Boulevard, c. 1965. The Hier brothers, Bob (facing camera) and Alan, race on the carousel horses at Uncle Ben's. Older brother Jim Hier recalls that Uncle Ben's was a popular place for birthday parties. Among its rides were a Big Eli Ferris Wheel No. 12 and an Allan Herschell Little Dipper coaster. (Ed and Ann Hier family.)

It Spells K-I-D-D-Y-L-A-N-D. Perhaps justifying its frequent relocations, Uncle Ben's (rather long) slogan was, "Please remember: No matter where you live or how far you have to drive, every child's heart . . . every child's home is close to Uncle Ben's Kiddyland." (HC/OCA.)

OUT-OF-THIS-WORLD FIGHTER JETS, 1951. At a children's carnival or park in the San Fernando Valley, brothers Bob and Phil Hermann experience atomic-age thrills in a streamlined two-seater rocket—possibly a Herschell Sky Fighter—equipped with swiveling guns on each side. (RH.)

ANOTHER C.W. PARKER CAROUSEL. At one time, picturesque Fairmount Park in Riverside had a beautiful lake and boathouse, a miniature golf course, a pool, a children's amusement park, a zoo, and a train ride. By the 1970s, the park was in decline. Recent efforts have restored some parts of the historic park, although the carousel was relocated to Flint, Michigan. (Courtesy of the Museum of Riverside.)

KIDDIELAND IN SAN DIEGO, 1947. Two boys hunker into the cockpits of drop-tank planes at a San Diego area children's amusement park. In 1948, Happy Hollow opened at Highland Avenue and Division Street in National City with a Toonerville trolley, Ferris wheel, and a 16-mm mini-theater. That same year, there was also a Tiny Town and a Playland on El Cajon Boulevard; kiddielands were booming in California's southernmost corner.

LITTLE DIPPER, SCANDIA FAMILY FUN PARK. A small chain of Scandinavian-themed amusement centers closed its Ontario park in 2019 after 27 years in operation. Scandia is a modern-day family park with several child-sized rides, a miniature golf course, a giant slide, and a racetrack. (Fred Nure.)

Two

WESTERN-THEMED PARKS

Among its many firsts, Knott's Berry Farm was Southern California's original Western-themed park. Walter Knott's Ghost Town Village and Covered Wagon Show were introduced in the 1940s to entertain patrons waiting for tables at Mrs. Knott's Chicken Dinner Restaurant. A few years later, television was the new frontier, and Western B-movies ruled the airwaves with a new generation of viewers who saw cowboys and Native Americans as superheroes. Western-themed television series like *The Lone Ranger* and local shows followed, hosted by cowboy stars like Doye O'Dell and Monte Hall. Southern California Western singers performed on television, in clubs, and made appearances at parades and amusement parks throughout the Southland. It was the 1950s, and Westerns ruled the range.

Even better, most of the movies and TV series were filmed in Southern California so families could get an up-close look at stunt choreography and on-location filming. Corriganville, a working movie ranch, was open on weekends and special occasions to provide a stroll through the dusty streets of the shooting location for *Death Valley Days*, *Gunsmoke*, and *Bonanza*, among others. Stunt performers and guest actors recreated action scenes with duels, horses, and stagecoaches. Friendly ranch owner/actor/stuntman Ray "Crash" Corrigan posed for photographs and made sure everyone had a rip-roarin' time.

Wildly popular William Boyd, also known as Hopalong Cassidy, opened a short-lived amusement park in Venice in 1951. The Newport Harbor Buffalo Ranch offered 115 acres filled with roaming bison, along with burro and pony rides, and—perhaps a forerunner of Lion Country Safari—visitors could drive through the ranch to view the woolly mammals.

Some kiddielands from San Diego to Los Angeles transformed into Western-themed parks or added props and pony rides to cash in on the cowboy craze. El Cajon's Wagonwheel Playland became Marshal Scotty's Playland Park, entertaining locals for decades. In 1946, Beverly Park proprietor David Bradley added a Hurlbut steam train and, later, pony carts that passed through a small Western town. When Disneyland opened in 1955, Frontierland was one of five original themed lands. Early attractions there included the Rainbow Caverns Mine Train and Conestoga Wagons.

A Cowboy Superstar. In the late 1940s, actor William Boyd had the foresight to obtain all rights to the Hopalong Cassidy character he portrayed in earlier films. Boyd sold his ranch and car, saved, borrowed, and scraped together $350,000. After signing 1,500 contracts, the rights to Hoppy were Boyd's, and he started a highly profitable franchise. (UWWBC.)

Hoppy Mania: America's First TV Hero. In his mid-50s, Boyd hit the peak of his career. As Hopalong Cassidy, he hosted television shows featuring his character's movies. More than 2,500 licensed products bore the Hopalong Cassidy name, including cowboy clothes for kids, comics, games, lunch boxes, and even canned tuna. Along with his horse, Topper, Boyd was mobbed at guest appearances and parades throughout the country. (UWWBC.)

HOPPYLAND OF VENICE. In 1951, Boyd signed on as co-owner of a children's cowboy-themed amusement park in Venice. Hoppyland replaced the short-lived Venice Lake Park and featured 20 adult and children's rides, including ponies, a Toonerville trolley, a Little Dipper roller coaster, an animal carousel, and two Ferris wheels. (UWWBC.)

NOW OPEN — 25-ACRE PICNIC GROUNDS
Hoppy's Horse in person . . . Hundreds of exciting things to see and do for the WHOLE FAMILY.

80-ACRE **HOPPYLAND**

West's highest Ferris Wheel, Zeppelin Sky Ride, Boat Rides, Pony Rides, Miniature Auto Races, Merry-Go-Rounds, Roller Coaster, Kiddieland . . . **400 WEST WASHINGTON ST. VENICE, CALIF.**
OPEN WEEK DAYS Noon Till 11 P.M. 10 ACRES OF PARKING
SAT. & SUN. 10 A.M. TILL MIDNITE. Come Today!

EIGHTY ACRES OF FUN. During Hoppyland's three-year existence, Boyd made frequent appearances at the park, reminding children to respect their parents, be honest and thrifty, work hard, and drink their milk. Hoppyland closed in 1954, with the property becoming part of Marina Del Rey in the 1960s. (Pictorial Press Ltd / Alamy Stock Photo.)

ACTION ON THE STREETS OF SILVERTOWN. Stunt shows like this shootout were staged throughout the park to give visitors an inside look at how their favorite Westerns were filmed, showing off the actors' mastery with fake guns, fist-fighting, and special effects. More than 3,500 movies and television series were filmed there. (BA.)

MORE THAN A FACADE. Corriganville's Silver Dollar Saloon was one of several actual working buildings and served 5¢ beer (for adults) and salami sandwiches. Beyond its Silvertown, Frontier Cafe, and shops, Corriganville featured lots to do and explore, like rodeos, archery, lakes, caves, mines, cabins, a fort, and a Mexican village, along with horseback and boat rides. (BA.)

THE CORRIGANVILLE YOUNG GUNS. Children like Evan Biren (center) and his brother Matt (second from right) could act out their Old West daydreams at the sprawling movie ranch in the Santa Susana Mountains. During the 1950s, Corriganville was one of the top attractions in the Southland. (BF.)

ACTOR GILBERT ROLAND AND GANG. Gilbert Roland, the Mexican-born actor who starred as the heroic caballero in *The Cisco Kid* movies, was one of many actors who appeared at Corriganville. Others who showed up included Tom Mix, Tex Ritter, Robert Taylor, and the stars of television's *Space Patrol*. (The Pierce family.)

THE OLD WEST WAS NOT "GUYS ONLY." Western stunt shows featuring men, women, and children were staged in the dusty streets of Silvertown and in the 4,000-seat arena and included bank robberies, stagecoach holdups, and gunfights. A full-time researcher wove historically accurate Old West details into the shows and stunts at Corriganville. (GMA.)

COWGIRL COUSINS WITH CORRIGAN. Merle Klekner (left) and Carol O'Connor get a boost from Crash Corrigan himself in 1952. Corriganville closed its wrought-iron gates in 1965, and two separate fires in the 1970s destroyed most of Silvertown. Corriganville became the infamous Spahn Ranch for the Quentin Tarantino film *Once Upon a Time in Hollywood.* (Michael Klekner.)

NEWPORT HARBOR BUFFALO RANCH. In 1954, building contractor Gene Clark shipped 72 buffalo from his Kansas ranch to the rolling hills of South Orange County. Leasing the land from the Irvine Co., Clark outfitted his 115-acre Buffalo Ranch with a trading post, restaurant, barns, and a petting zoo. The ranch was about a mile inland from the coast. (OCA.)

TECHNICALLY, THEY WERE BISON. A precursor to the following decade's nearby Lion Country Safari, Buffalo Ranch offered a drive-through look at the beasts. Large hay bales created barriers to keep the animals grazing within at least 10 feet from the road. Visitors were cautioned not to leave their vehicles or annoy the buffalo. (OCA.)

TEPEES AT THE ENTRANCE. Hoping to bring an educational and cultural experience to the community, Clark invited people from various Native American tribes to form a "village" at the ranch. Dressed in traditional clothing, Native Americans presented dances, storytelling, crafts, and rituals. (OCA.)

BUFFALO BURGERS CAME FROM THE HERD. Gene Clark, right, chuckles as Guy Norris "Texas Tiny" Cherry, an entertainer known as the "World's Largest Cowboy," takes a chomp of a buffalo burger at the silo-shaped on-site cafe. As Texas Tiny, Cherry hosted a morning show on local radio station KFOX, was a bandleader, and a cast member of the country-western television show *Town Hall Party.* (OCA.)

LARGEST BUFFALO RANCH IN THE WORLD. Or at least in California, since nobody seemed to dispute the claim. Up until the Buffalo Ranch opened its gates, much of the land owned by the Irvine Co. was used for cattle and to grow crops like lima beans, olives, barley, and strawberries. To bring in more revenue, horse shows and barbecues were held during the ranch's four-year existence. (OCA.)

ANOTHER WAY TO VIEW THE HERD. For Old West authenticity, visitors could gaze at the bison from one of the ranch's stagecoaches, which was a bumpy but memorable journey through the dusty hills. Buffalo Ranch also had a train, burro and pony rides, and a fire engine. (OCA.)

LAST STOP, BUFFALO GULCH. Competition from Disneyland and financial issues forced Clark to close Buffalo Ranch in 1959. In 1961, some of the buildings became offices for William Pereira, the acclaimed Modernist architect who master-planned the city of Irvine and designed several buildings for the University of California, Irvine (UCI). (OCA.)

TINY TOWN ROUGH RIDERS. In the early 1950s, the Compton kiddieland took on a Western theme. Owner Harry "Matt" Matthews used his public relations skills to lasso local country music and television stars for weekend appearances that were advertised in area newspapers. (TTP.)

CAROLINA COTTON, THE GIRL OF THE GOLDEN WEST. Cotton was a singer, actress, local television host, and savvy businesswoman who had her name above the sign of Tiny Town for a couple of years as a marketing co-venture with Matthews. The vivacious yodeler participated in activities at the park and was an accomplished horseback rider. (CCE.)

TOURED WITH BOB WILLS, SONS OF THE PIONEERS. At Tiny Town, Carolina Cotton engaged with fans on weekends, then hosted KTTV's *Hometown Hayride* on Saturday evenings. After the war, country music topped the charts from San Diego to Bakersfield, and local television shows hosted by Western Swing personalities ruled the ratings. (CCE.)

DOYE O'DELL'S TINY TOWN. Like Cotton, O'Dell was a country singer and actor and had his name briefly above Tiny Town and Lucas Kiddieland. Locally, O'Dell was voted Outstanding Child's TV Entertainer and hosted KTLA's popular *Cowboy Thrills* television show. He also had his own brand of popcorn. (The O'Dell family.)

MATT MATTHEWS AND IRON EYES CODY. Numerous stars appeared at Tiny Town, including Stan Freberg, Uncle Archie, Skipper Frank, and Roscoe Ates. Born Espera Oscar de Corti to Sicilian immigrant parents, Iron Eyes Cody starred in more than 200 films and television series and wore his Native American costumes in everyday life. In the early 1970s, Cody appeared in the popular television ad "Keep America Beautiful" as the crying Native American. (TTP.)

FRONTIER TOWN, SEVEN MILES FROM EL CAJON. The Old West–themed park in San Diego County's Dehesa opened in 1962 and joined forces with nearby Big Oak Ranch around 1970. The remote park on Harbison Canyon Road featured a steam train, stagecoach rides, a carousel, pony rides, staged shootouts, and a Western town with shops, a doll museum, and restaurants.

BIG OAK RANCH, THE 1970s. Children perch on an Old West wagon with Frontier Town behind them. Under the new ownership of Herman "Rock" Kreutzer, the ranch became a venue for events and concerts through the mid-1980s. Locals recall seeing performers like Buck Owens, Merle Haggard, and Waylon Jennings. But, in 1985, owner Kreutzer was convicted and imprisoned for second-degree murder; shortly thereafter, the park closed. (The May family/ Vintage San Diego.)

MONTE HALL, SAN DIEGO TV HOST. Host of the KFMB television series *Channel 8 Corral*, Western singer and actor Monte Hall celebrated children's birthdays, and talented locals became part of his ranch crew. Hall (not to be confused with the game show host) also owned Monte Hall's Playland, a Western kiddieland on El Cajon Boulevard, in the 1950s. (Kelli Mallard.)

RICKEY HILL AT MONTE HALL'S PLAYLAND.
Hall held talent shows at Playland on
Sundays; musical and dancing standouts
were invited to perform on his TV show
the following weekend. The park included
pony rides, a Ferris wheel, and appearances
by Hall and his horse, Comanche. In
the late 1950s, Hall hosted *Tiny Town
Ranch* on KFMB. Sadly, he died of a
stroke in December 1959. (Rick Hill.)

THE MOST-REMEMBERED PARK. Starting in the 1950s as Scotty's Wagon Wheel Playland and
Marshal Scotty's Playland, the Western-themed park evolved into Marshal Scotty's in the ensuing
decades and entertained generations of San Diegans. While it had a roller coaster, water slide,
Ferris wheel, and go-carts, many fondly remember celebrating birthdays and riding the ponies.
(Tamera Rankin Kwist.)

INDIAN VILLAGE INTRODUCED IN THE MID-1950S. The Knott family had an extremely successful Chicken Dinner Restaurant starting in the 1930s before adding its Calico Ghost Town. Little Joel Weber (left) imitates a stoic chief while his sister, Julia (right), is not too happy about the situation. (The Weber family.)

PACK MULES THROUGH NATURE'S WONDERLAND. In 1960, Disneyland revamped its Frontierland mule ride as an E-ticket tour through the fictitious town of Rainbow Ridge and a Disney vision of the Old West. The mules carried passengers through 1973. (NDF.)

Three

ANIMAL-THEMED PARKS

During the mid-20th century, most zoos, aquariums, and wildlife habitats were built for entertainment. Dancing bears, dolphins leaping through rings, and pantomiming chimps enthralled visitors and audiences at the zoos and parks popping up throughout Southern California. Griffith Park Zoo operated from 1912 until 1966, when it was replaced by the 133-acre Los Angeles Zoo and Botanical Gardens. Proving Los Angeles was, indeed, a mecca for the offbeat, the Los Angeles Alligator Farm operated in Lincoln Park from 1907 to 1953, when it relocated to Buena Park near Knott's Berry Farm.

Jungleland in Thousand Oaks was a reincarnation of Goebel's Lion Farm, first as the World Jungle Compound in 1946 and then as Jungleland when two 20th Century Fox executives bought it in 1956 with visions of turning it into a Disneyland with live animals. The park featured a petting zoo, shows with big-name trainers, and rides.

Orange County was home to two of the more unusual animal theme parks: the Japanese Village and Deer Park in Buena Park and Lion Country Safari in Irvine. Both were strategically located near Disneyland and Knott's Berry Farm, joining the growing number of parks in the county that helped it become a top family vacation destination. Besides deer, the Buena Park attraction offered shows with seals, bears, and dolphins, along with Japanese cultural demonstrations of tea ceremonies, karate, and dancing. Lion Country Safari was a new breed of theme parks: visitors drove through in their cars (or chartered buses) to view wild animals in their native habitat, which was Irvine's interpretation of the African Serengeti.

While the American Society for the Prevention of Cruelty to Animals dates back to 1866, it took more than a century to realize its goals of animal rescue, placement, and protection. In the ensuing decades, other animal rights and welfare organizations have been formed, including the World Association of Zoos and Aquariums (WAZA) and People for the Ethical Treatment of Animals (PETA). It is likely that many of the postwar animal parks would have had to undergo drastic reformation if they were to continue to operate.

THE LOS ANGELES ALLIGATOR FARM. Tourists and locals interacted with the exotic reptiles in Lincoln Park, posing and "riding" on top of them, along with marveling at the alligators' antics, like crawling up a ramp and sliding down shoots into ponds. Since Hollywood was nearby, some alligators were used in the *Tarzan* movies and other films. Billy, the park's largest alligator, weighed 800 pounds and was 13.5 feet long. (The Ward family.)

A MOVE TO BUENA PARK. In November 1953, the farm was renamed the California Alligator Farm and relocated from Lincoln Heights to Buena Park, across the street from Knott's Berry Farm, starting a trend of amusement parks and attractions clustering near bigger theme parks. Its 1,000 alligators and numerous reptiles continued to frighten and fascinate visitors until the farm closed in 1984. Many of the reptiles retired to Florida. (OCA.)

ROB STARKMAN AT BEVERLY PONYLAND. Next door to Beverly Park was Ponyland, which was opened in 1945 by Leo and Viva Murphy. When it was announced that Beverly Center would be built on the lot, widow Viva said she wanted to keep a few Shetlands. "I've been with the ponies so long they feel like family," she told the *Los Angeles Times* in 1978. (SFA.)

WELCOME TO JUNGLE GARDENS OF ANAHEIM. In 1953, wild animal-lovers Jack and Dorothy Dutton opened a small zoo, tropical restaurant, beauty parlor, and gift shop at their five-acre compound. Among the 400 exotic birds and various beasts was the star of Jungle Gardens: Jerry, the "world's most human" chimp. Jerry was part of the family and could brush his teeth and dress himself. (Sign image, Fullerton Public Library; inset, Anaheim Public Library.)

THE PALMS RESTAURANT AT JUNGLE GARDENS. Patrons of the swanky Palms rendezvoused in the Terrace Room or Lantern Bar while chimpanzee Jerry dined on steak with ketchup followed by an after-supper smoke. Zoo visitors were captivated by the caged monkeys and birds surrounded by lush palms, banana trees, and bamboo. Jerry helped water the gardens and entertained all with his boyish antics. The Jungle closed in the mid-1970s. (The Anaheim Public Library.)

FINAL YEARS OF THE GRIFFITH PARK ZOO. Founded in 1912, the zoo led a rocky existence before closing to make way for the new and improved Los Angeles Zoo and Botanical Gardens, which opened two miles away in 1966. During the Works Progress Administration (WPA) in the 1930s, 12,000 were employed to improve the zoo grounds and other Los Angeles parks, building seven grottoes and five heated cat cages. (UCIWG.)

ENTRANCE, JAPANESE VILLAGE AND DEER PARK. Located on Knott Avenue in Buena Park, the attraction opened its *torii* gates in 1967 and was inspired by Japan's Nara Park. Described as a place of relaxation, visitors could stroll among the 300 deer, koi ponds, pearl divers, and a teahouse that served sushi, noodles, and hot dogs. (SFA.)

ENCLOSED DOVE PAVILION. Doves are known for their peaceful and gentle nature, which made them a popular attraction at the deer park. Visitors loved to pose with doves perched on their arms or shoulders along with hostesses outfitted in traditional silk kimonos. Allen Parkinson, who made his fortune with Sleep-Eze, dreamed up the deer park, Movieland, and the Palace of Living Art. (Bob Henry.)

ROB STARKMAN WITH CHITAL DEER. The 30-acre park was populated with English fallow and Japanese Sika deer that congregated by the vending machines. For a nickel, visitors could buy a handful of special crackers to satiate the eager deer. Signs warned, "Caution: Deer May Nibble Clothing and the Park Cannot be Responsible for Soiling." (SFA)

PERFORMING PORPOISES, SEA THEATRE. The mid-20th century was an era when aquatic animal acts drew crowds to regional amusement parks. Porpoises jumping through rings of fire were perilous acts typical of animal theme park entertainment. The deer park claimed that its Sea Theatre featured the "world's largest man-made body of saltwater." (OCA.)

IN THE SHADOW OF THE NABISCO BUILDING. While nearby Knott's and Disneyland offered rides and nonstop entertainment, the Japanese Village and Deer Park was more of a peaceful place to admire the gardens and many bridges and koi ponds. Guests were entertained with shows and cultural demonstrations like traditional tea ceremonies, karate demonstrations, dance performances, and assorted animal acts. (OCA.)

SHRINKING ATTENDANCE, UNPROFITABILITY. The deer park closed on December 2, 1974. A week later, 177 deer were euthanized after testing positive for tuberculosis. The public became outraged: the Orange County Health Department reported that the tuberculosis (TB) strain was not transmissible to humans nor always fatal to deer. Nearby Lion Country Safari offered to take the remaining deer, but they were later transported to the UC Davis School of Veterinary Medicine for a TB study funded by Six Flags, reported the *Los Angeles Times*. (OCA.)

ENCHANTED VILLAGE REPLACES JAPANESE VILLAGE. Spearheaded by animal trainer Ralph Hefler, Enchanted Village was a gentle jungle with aquatic shows and "happenings" throughout the 32-acre park, like a woman playing guitar on a grassy knoll with a lion at her feet or a man covered in tarantulas. Despite attractions like the Bicentennial Tribute to Animals and a mythical aquatic swampland show, the park lasted one year, closing in 1977. (OCA.)

JUNGLELAND USA OF THOUSAND OAKS. When two 20th Century Fox executives bought the Old World Jungle Compound in 1957, plans were announced to transform it into a theme park with rides, shows, and safaris that would rival Disneyland. The compound opened as Goebel's Lion Farm in 1926 and was an animal training center, zoo, and amusement park. Although it was sold several times, the Goebel family always ended up reacquiring it. (CTL.)

THE MAGNIFICENT MABEL STARK. The fearless first female tiger trainer landed in Hollywood after years of touring with circuses throughout the world. Stark stunt doubled for Mae West in the film *I'm No Angel*. She worked at Goebel's and Jungleland for 30 years and survived a few maulings during her long career. "It doesn't take brute force to train brutes," the diminutive blonde once told a reporter. "Nearly everyone who doesn't know that expects me to be a strapping woman of 200 pounds with a heavy hand and a deep, hypnotic scowl."

PAT ANTHONY, FAMOUS TRAINER. The first World War II veteran to study wild animal training under the GI Bill, Anthony apprenticed at the compound in Thousand Oaks. The handsome trainer was also a stunt double in films with wild animals, including *Samson and Delilah* and *The River of No Return*. Audiences at Jungleland witnessed Anthony using barrel rolls (pictured), balls, chairs, and flat whips in his riveting act. (UCIWG.)

KAREN ROBERTSON WITH A RABBIT. Happy Karen snuggles a bunny at Jungleland's petting zoo around 1965. The compound was open for student field trips and featured two animal training sessions on weekdays and continuous shows on weekends. In the mid-1960s, Jungleland's draw was its celebrity animals, including shows with stars of the 1967 film *Doctor Doolittle*. (CTL/MJR.)

BIRTHDAY PARTIES AT JUNGLELAND. Some lucky locals—like Debbie Birenbaum (with the camera), second from left—celebrated their birthdays at Jungleland and were entertained by the animals, Randy Runyon (wearing hat), and Chucko the clown. For decades, Goebel's and Jungleland were out in the country, 40 miles from Los Angeles. Postwar suburban sprawl caught up to it, making the land more valuable. After bankruptcy forced closure in 1969, the Thousand Oaks Civic Arts Plaza was built on the site. (CTL/DB.)

TINA MASON FEEDS A FRIEND. The singer was at Jungleland with pop star Keith Allison shooting the Dick Clark television series *Where the Action Is* in the mid-1960s. Other television shows and films shot there included the *Tarzan* movie series, *The Fugitive*, and *Route 66*. In 1966, Jayne Mansfield's six-year-old son, Zoltán Hargitay, was mauled by a "tame" lion while visiting Jungleland. Hargitay survived, but Mansfield sued. Bankruptcy and theme park competition reportedly contributed to the park's closure. (CTL/HN.)

ENTRANCE, LION COUNTRY SAFARI. The first Lion Country Safari African Preserve opened in South Florida in 1967, followed three years later by the Orange County compound, which was located on land owned by the Irvine Co. The entrance with the familiar tusk archway was at 8800 Moulton Parkway, which is now Irvine Center and Research Drives. The cageless zoo charged per-person admission fees. (Vic Bennett.)

INTERACTION WITH WILDLIFE. The animals' unpredictability was part of the park's appeal. Visitors recall lions leaping into truck beds, monkeys jumping up and down on car hoods and peeling off plastic bumpers, and ostriches or giraffes blocking the road. Rangers patrolled the preserve in zebra-striped Jeeps. (OCA.)

Traffic-Stopping Cheetahs. If visitors were lucky, they would encounter a coalition of cheetahs or a mob of emus cavorting a few feet from their car. Other animals roaming the preserve included elephants, rhinoceros, hippopotamuses, zebra, chimpanzees (a perennial favorite of Southern California parks), antelopes, and birds. Not surprisingly, convertibles were not permitted. (OCA.)

View from the Car. Some visitors took stunning photos of the wildlife with professional cameras, resulting in African safari-caliber images that were actually the dry hills of Irvine. Not all cars (especially older models) had air-conditioning, but visitors were warned to keep windows rolled up and not exit their vehicles, so the views were as wide and clear as car windows. Of course, not everyone followed the rules and threw dry bread and other treats from their vehicles to lure the beasts closer. (Joost van Beek collection.)

FRASIER, THE SENSUOUS LION. The star of Lion Country Safari was an elderly lion rescued from a Mexican circus. Frasier was thin, mangy, arthritic, and missing teeth, which caused his tongue to droop. His vitamin-enriched diet or laid-back personality appealed to seven lionesses, who quickly abandoned the resident males to form a pride after Frasier's arrival and showed their affection by bringing him choice cuts of meat. (The Irvine Historical Society.)

EMPLOYEE VICKI ANDERSON WITH A CUB. About 85 in human years, Frasier sired 35 cubs in 18 months. The subject of light-news stories and the butt of talk-show jokes, Frasier became a media sensation and boosted park attendance by 15 percent. The virile lion spawned a movie, a song recorded by Sarah Vaughan, apparel, and bumper stickers. Unfortunately, Frasier died in 1972 of pneumonia. His legacies are a bronze plaque and a commemorative oak tree on the former grounds. (The Irvine Historical Society.)

HIPPO BOATS ON LAKE SHANALEE. Not just confined to vehicles, Lion Country Safari visitors could stretch their legs and get more of an amusement park experience at the Safari Camp and entertainment area. Attractions included the Afritheatre, Native Villages, and the Zambezi River Cruise. In 1981, Irvine Meadows Amphitheater (later Verizon Wireless) opened on part of the safari grounds. Designed by Gin Wong Associates, the amphitheater closed and was razed in 2016. (Vic Bennett.)

JUNIOR JUNGLE "PETTING ZOO." For a hands-on experience, children like Anthony and Vanessa Strode could play with babies or "tame" older animals. Another park animal made headlines when Bubbles the hippo escaped in 1978 and died from a potent tranquilizer dart, according to a 2009 *Orange County Register* article. In 1983, Misty, a performing elephant, broke loose and killed a park zoologist. The four-ton pachyderm was tranquilized and later sold to a Chicago circus. Lion Country closed in 1984 partially due to declining attendance. (The Strode family.)

59

OLD MACDONALD'S FARM, KNOTT'S. Owned by Kay and Fulton Shaw, the animal farm/petting zoo concession opened at Knott's Berry Farm in 1953 and entertained guests for 15 years with an assortment of trained rabbits, chickens, goats, pigs, and other domesticated animals. The Seal Pool (pictured) was just outside the petting zoo's entrance. Visitors could buy sardines and watch the pinnipeds dive and catch the fish. There was also a section to hold birthday parties. In 1970, the Shaws moved the farm to the new master-planned community of Mission Viejo.

OVERHEAD OF THE NEW OLD MACDONALD'S. The farm relocated to Mission Viejo, just off the 5 Freeway and Crown Valley Parkway in a seven-acre hollow now occupied by the Kaleidoscope. The property had an old farmhouse, barn, outbuildings, and mature trees on-site, which made it an ideal setup for the Shaws to continue Old MacDonald's Farm. The new location offered more room for the children and the horses, mules, and other animals to roam. (MVCHCC.)

HORSE-POWERED CAROUSEL SWING. A popular ride with children at Old MacDonald's was a two- or three-person swing carousel attached by wooden beams in the center, operated by a horse that was guided by farmhands. Other attractions included a Pavlovian-trained menagerie that included a Russian bear, sliding pigs, exotic chickens, and cattle. It was a great place to hold birthdays, with cake, ice cream, and conical hats, along with the tractor-pulled tram ride. (Bob Read.)

VINTAGE WAGON, MISSION VIEJO. Something as basic as climbing on old farm equipment entertained children at Old MacDonald's. Locals fondly recall goats bleating from the roof of the barn and a piano-playing chicken. The place was not slick, and the rides were simple, all of which were part of its charm. (MVCHCC.)

PALM SPRINGS TRAMWAY ANIMAL PARK. Dolphins in the desert? In 1968, a zoo was built behind the Palm Springs Aerial Tramway. Attractions included deer, baboons, a monkey that danced to the jazz hit "The Stripper," and a macaw high-wire act. Financial crises, personnel transitions, and lawsuits forced name changes: from the Palm Springs Aerial Tramway Animal Park to Animal World to Circus Animal Land. Local headlines about hungry animals and excessive heat prompted citizens to assist. In August 1969, Palm Springs recorded a then-record high of 120 degrees Fahrenheit. The Bavarian-themed zoo closed in September 1970. The dolphins were relocated to SeaWorld.

Four

THEMED PARKS AND ROADSIDE ATTRACTIONS

During 1971's soft economy, the Buena Park Chamber of Commerce sent an employee to work at San Francisco International Airport. Her job was to lure Northern Californians to Orange County to visit the numerous amusement parks and attractions. The county was recognized as the amusement capital of the United States and was home to the first and third most popular man-made facilities in the world: Disneyland and Knott's Berry Farm, respectively. With the instantaneous, overwhelming success of Disneyland in 1955, amusement park designers, developers, and investors—ranging from untested to experienced—scrambled to come up with something new.

In some cases, park owners got imaginative and downright bizarre. Others could not define a theme, so their parks became like those restaurants that offer too many choices but specialize in nothing. Some parks and attractions merited one visit and then could be checked off the to-do list. For others, themes crossed over: biblical, dinosaur, and three wax museums in one county.

Then there were the parks that were planned but never realized. For decades, Long Beach has been a place of amusement park dreams that were bigger than what was built. It was announced in 1964 that the California World's Fair would be held in Long Beach in 1967–1968, with Charles Luckman Associates master-planning the project. It never happened, but Expo 67 in Montreal did. In 1974, the Long Beach City Council approved the development of Pleasure Island, a 475-acre movie park near the *Queen Mary* to be themed around Irwin Allen, the "Master of Disaster" producer responsible for movies like *The Poseidon Adventure* and *The Towering Inferno*. Marine explorer Jacques Cousteau tried twice to expand his *Queen Mary* exhibit, The Living Sea, into an amusement park in Long Beach or Huntington Beach. Architect Frank Gehry drew plans in 1967 for a proposed Watts Automotive Amusement Park.

Numerous water parks made a splash and then sank. One of the first aquatic-themed destinations planned was Spade Cooley's Water World near Tehachapi in 1960, but his conviction and incarceration for murdering his wife put an end to an already-tanking project. The Mojave Desert's Lake Dolores lasted for years and then became Rock-a-Hoola and Discover Waterpark. Photographs of its ruins are popular to post on social media. Wild Rivers in Irvine lasted for 25 years on land once inhabited by Lion Country Safari. In true Southern California spirit, everyone waits for the next big idea.

MOTELS NEAR THEME PARKS. When Southern California became destination central in the 1950s, motels sprouted along main thoroughfares and promoted their proximity to amusement parks and attractions. To compete, they offered perks like "Free TV" and swimming pools. If that did not draw guests, then intriguing, amusement park-like names would do the trick: who could not resist the Peter Pan, Stovall's Space-Age, or the Park-Vue?

MOVIELAND WAX MUSEUM. The mastermind behind Movieland was Allen Parkinson, who later created the Japanese Village and Deer Park. Parkinson was so impressed with Madame Tussaud's in London that he brought the idea to Buena Park, with top wax sculptors recreating movie stars and scenes. Designed by architect Jack J. Strickland, Movieland featured a curved portico with 10 chandeliers. Each time a wax figure was unveiled, the star was chauffeured to the museum in the Movieland gold Rolls Royce.

STAR-STUDDED PREMIERES. Crowds gathered outside Movieland for the reveal of celebrities' wax figures. Clockwise, from the upper left are Sophia Loren and owner Allen Parkinson, Natalie Wood, Gloria Swanson with her wax lookalike, Mexican actor Cantinflas and his doppelganger, Harold Lloyd, and Mary Pickford at Movieland's grand opening. Parkinson was on hand for most of Movieland's premieres.

DANNY THOMAS WITH "THAT GIRL!" The entertainer/humanitarian father of actress Marlo Thomas plants a kiss on the cheek of her television-character likeness at Movieland. Marlo attended the March 1971 unveiling of her wax figure and donated a pair of false eyelashes she wore as *That Girl!*'s Anne Marie. In 1976, Danny brought a busload of friends and family for the reveal of his own Movieland wax figure.

ROBERT REDFORD AND PAUL NEWMAN. Outfitted as the characters from their 1969 film *Butch Cassidy and the Sundance Kid*, these wax figures were among Movieland's better likenesses. To prepare a figure, artists took 3-D photographs of each actor to be sculpted, along with precise measurements. The sculptors worked from images of the scenes in which the performer would be depicted in the tableau. Costumes were donated or duplicated, and sets and props were copied down to the smallest detail.

FRANKENSTEIN AND THE FREYCHEK SISTERS. Movieland visitors got to pose for fun photographs with characters not on display, like bolt-necked Frankenstein. In 1970, Parkinson sold the museum to Six Flags Inc. Movieland closed its doors in 2005. The gallery was demolished along with the building in 2016. (Marc Eugene Ferguson.)

NANCY SINATRA, "WILD ANGELS." Sultry Sinatra made a dazzling addition to Movieland when her wax figure premiered in a scene from the 1966 film. Trends and popularity waxed and waned during the museum's 43 years. Stars and scenes were pulled and replaced with more current ones, while bodies and props were repurposed. After Sinatra's display was removed, a wax Arnold Schwarzenegger was affixed to the handlebars of her custom-made motorcycle for *The Terminator*.

PALACE OF LIVING ART. In April 1966, Parkinson opened another wax museum adjacent to Movieland. For visitors who could not travel the world, he hoped the Palace would bring top museums to Buena Park, with reproductions of famous statuary and 3-D interpretations of paintings. Among the exhibits were Alexandros of Antioch's *Venus de Milo*, Leonardo da Vinci in the act of painting *Mona Lisa*, and Vincent Van Gogh sitting in the *Bedroom at Arles* (pictured). (OCA.)

MICHELANGELO'S *DAVID* IN THE OC. A giant crane placed the 10-ton, 18-foot marble replica of *David* where visitors could admire his chiseled attributes in the courtyard of the Palace of Living Art. Indoors, smaller sculptures were positioned with lifelike replicas to give the experience of viewing a model posing for the artist and with the final masterpiece. Other lifelike recreations included Leonardo da Vinci's *The Last Supper* and Grant Wood's *American Gothic*.

WIDE WORLD IN WAX. Designed by Richard Tom and Jan Truskier in the New Formalism architectural style, the Anaheim museum opened in 1966. The wax figures originally appeared at the Seattle World's Fair in 1962 and the New York World's Fair in 1964–1965. The 200 figures were an eclectic mix, ranging from Superman, French favorites like Maurice Chevalier and Napoleon, and plans to add wax Pulitzer Prize winners. (OCA.)

Welcome to Wide World in Wax . one block south of Disneyland

ED SULLIVAN

LADY GODIVA RIDES BAREBACK. The long-tressed wax maiden was on full display at the New York World's Fair before arriving in Anaheim. Wax museums close, and figures get sold, which is why collections sometimes appear out of sync, like the Beatles around the corner from Nimrod and some Parisian floozies in a champagne-fueled street fight. Anaheim's Wide World in Wax barely lasted two years before becoming a restaurant and then a Holiday Inn. (OCA.)

69

MORE WAX, C. 1966. Mission San Juan Capistrano visitors crossed the street to the Mission Wax Museum. Figures included Pres. John F. and Jacqueline Kennedy (left), Alice in Wonderland (upper right), and Charlie Chaplin (lower right). Added later were sports legends and Communist leaders. (OCA.)

MOVIE WORLD IN BUENA PARK. Opened in 1970, Movie World featured an array of movie props, celebrity memorabilia, historic and custom cars, and funhouse activities like a Chamber of Horrors, a rolling barrel, and a giant fun tube. Included in the collection were Robby the Robot from the 1956 film *Forbidden Planet* (far left), a 1914 Lozier (upper right), and custom cars by counterculture artist Ed "Big Daddy" Roth (lower right). (OCA.)

MOVIE WORLD RESTRUCTURES. In 1973, Movie World rebranded itself as Movie World Cars of the Stars and Planes of Fame. Besides a dinosaur egg from *Planet of the Apes* and 750 radiator ornaments, Movie World housed more than 600 vehicles. Among cars exhibited were two from the 1965 film *The Great Race*: the Hannibal 8 (right) and the Leslie Special (left). Major car auctions were held at Movie World until it closed in 1979. (OCA.)

TED CONIBEAR'S BIBLE LAND, 1965. From his home near Temecula, artist Conibear created Biblescapes using wet sand. It took 20 tons of sand and six months to create *The Last Supper* (pictured). In 1970, Conibear moved his exhibition to cover six acres near the 10 Freeway in Calimesa. Several times the artist quietly repaired his work after vandalisms. Conibear's family removed Bible Land after he died in 1994; in his absence, the statues deteriorated, and they believed only he could repair them. (William and Helen Hofmann.)

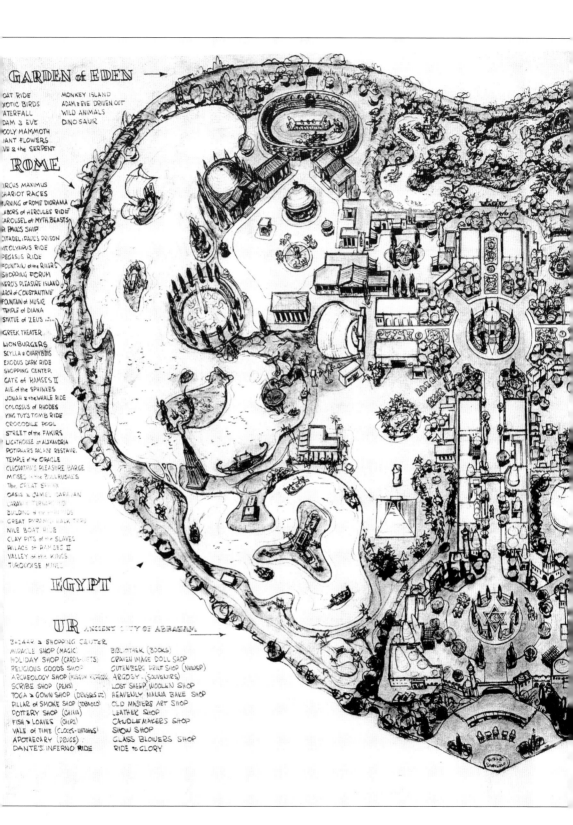

GARDEN of EDEN →

OAT RIDE
XOTIC BIRDS
ATERFALL
DAM & EVE
OOLY MAMMOTH
IANT FLOWERS
VE & the SERPENT

MONKEY ISLAND
ADAM & EVE DRIVEN OUT
WILD ANIMALS
DINOSAUR

ROME

IRCUS MAXIMUS
HARIOT RACES
URNING of ROME DIORAMA
ABORS of HERCULES RIDE
AROUSEL of MYTH BEASTS
 t PAUL'S SHIP
CITADEL: PAUL'S PRISON
NT OLYMPUS RIDE
PEGASUS RIDE
FOUNTAIN of the RIVERS
SHOPPING FORUM
NERO'S PLEASURE ISLAND
ARCH of CONSTANTINE
FOUNTAIN of MUSIC
TEMPLE of DIANA
STATUE of ZEUS ......

GREEK THEATER
LIONBURGERS
SKYLLA & CHARYBDIS
EXODUS DARK RIDE
SHOPPING CENTER
GATE of RAMSES II
AVE. of the SPHINXES
JONAH & the WHALE RIDE
COLOSSUS of RHODES
KING TUT'S TOMB RIDE
CROCODILE POOL
STREET of the FAKIRS
LIGHTHOUSE at ALEXANDRIA
POTIPHAR'S PALACE RESTAUR.
TEMPLE of the ORACLE
CLEOPATRA'S PLEASURE BARGE
MOSES in the BULLRUSHES
The GREAT SPHINX
OASIS & CAMEL CARAVAN
CARAVAN TURNER RID
BUILDING of the PYRAMIDS
GREAT PYRAMID WALK THRU
NILE BOAT RIDE
CLAY PITS of the SLAVES
PALACE of RAMSES II
VALLEY of the KINGS
TURQUOISE MINES

EGYPT

UR ANCIENT CITY of ABRAHAM →

BAZAAR & SHOPPING CENTER
MIRACLE SHOP (MAGIC)
HOLIDAY SHOP (CARDS-GIFTS)
RELIGIOUS GOODS SHOP
ARCHEOLOGY SHOP (MUSEUM REPROS)
SCRIBE SHOP (PENS)
TOGA & GOWN SHOP (DRESSES ET)
PILLAR of SMOKE SHOP (TOBACCO)
POTTERY SHOP (CHINA)
FISH & LOAVES (CHIPS)
VALE of TIME (CLOCKS-WATCHES)
APOTHECARY (DRUGS)
DANTE'S INFERNO RIDE

BIBLIOTHEK (BOOKS)
GRAVEN IMAGE DOLL SHOP
GUTENBERG PRINT SHOP (NEWSP)
ARGOSY (SOUVENIRS)
LOST SHEEP WOOLEN SHOP
HEAVENLY MANNA BAKE SHOP
OLD MASTERS ART SHOP
LEATHER SHOP
CANDLE MAKERS SHOP
SHOE SHOP
GLASS BLOWERS SHOP
RIDE to GLORY

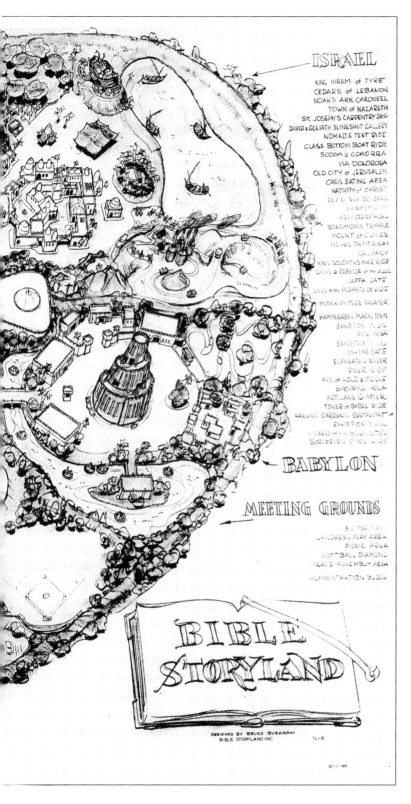

ISRAEL

KING HIRAM of TYRE
CEDARS of LEBANON
NOAH'S ARK CAROUSEL
TOWN of NAZARETH
ST. JOSEPH'S CARPENTRY SHOP
DAVID & GOLIATH SLINGSHOT GALLERY
NOMAD'S TENT RIDE
GLASS BOTTOM BOAT RIDE
SODOM & GOMORRA
VIA DOLOROSA
OLD CITY of JERUSALEM
OASIS EATING AREA
NATIVITY of CHRIST
DEAD SEA SCROLLS
CONVENT RIDE
HEROD'S CITADEL
SOLOMON'S TEMPLE
MOUNT of OLIVES
MOSES ON MT SINAI
CALVARY
KING SOLOMONS MINE RIDE
OASIS & REBECCA at the WELL
JAFFA GATE
LIVES of the PROPHETS DR RIDE

MOTION PICTURE THEATER

HAMMURABIS MAGIC TOWN
EXHIBITION BLDG.
RIDE AREA
EXHIBITION BLDG.
ISHTAR GATE
EUPHRATES RIVER
RIVER RIDE
AVE. of GOLD & SOUKE
SHOPPING AREA
ARTISANS QUARTER
TOWER of BABEL RIDE
HANGING GARDENS RESTAURANT
EXHIBITION BLDG.
ISLAND of the SCULPTORS
SORCERERS MAGIC RIDE

BABYLON

MEETING GROUNDS

BIG TOP TENT
CHILDREN'S PLAY AREA
PICNIC AREA
SOFTBALL DIAMOND
PARADE ASSEMBLY AREA

ADMINISTRATION BLDGS.

BIBLE STORYLAND

DESIGNED BY BRUCE BUSHMAN
BIBLE STORYLAND INC.   1L-8

BIBLE STORYLAND, RANCHO CUCAMONGA. Religious theme parks seemed like a divine idea. In 1960, Bible Storyland almost offered the masses 220 acres of rapture in the Inland Empire. Creator Nat Winecoff (who worked for Disney) and investors Jack Haley (*The Wizard of Oz's* Tin Man) and Donald Duncan (of yo-yos and parking meter fame) conceived an amusement that looked familiar. Six themed sections–the Garden of Eden, Ur, Israel, Egypt, Babylon, and Rome–would each contain glorious rides. The heart-shaped park was said to symbolize God's love of humanity, although many have noted its uncanny resemblance to the map of Disneyland. (BBHJ.)

73

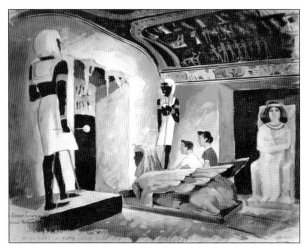

KING TUT'S TOMB RIDE. Former Disney artist Bruce Bushman designed the beautiful watercolor concepts and sketches that included Bible Storyland attractions like Ride to Glory, Jonah and the Whale, Noah's Ark, and Carousel of the Mythical Beasts. Alas, Bible Storyland's A Trip to Heaven, lionburgers, Dante's Inferno, and other joyful ideas were not meant to be. While bulldozers began moving earth on Foothill Boulevard, church representatives protested, calling the park a "blasphemous use of Holy Scriptures." (BBHJ.)

DINOSAURLAND, ALPINE, 1962. Visitors to the prehistoric-themed park in San Diego County enjoyed the Cavern Snack Bar, swimming pool, and picnic grounds, all in a forest of giant ferns, tropical plants, and boulders with "animated" prehistoric beasts. The triceratops stood 35 feet tall, towering over a 15-foot stegosaurus. Future plans included sea turtles, an erupting volcano, and a dinosaur dark ride. Dinosaurland lasted a couple of years before becoming a mobile home park with dinosaurs left intact. (Alpine Historical & Conservation Society.)

SANTA'S VILLAGE, SKYFOREST. In 1955, Santa's Village opened six weeks before Disneyland. The village's storybook architectural design was ideal for its mountain setting. Promotions and buzz obviously worked because opening day found an overflow of cars that some say backed down the winding road all the way to San Bernardino city limits. (RKC.)

SANTA AND ALAN LADD. The handsome actor and his family were invited guests on opening day at Santa's Village. Santa (Bill Strothers) pointed out some of the park's finer amenities to Ladd (right) while visitors did double-takes at the tan star of *Shane.* The two were standing in front of Santa's home, with its zany pocketwatch-shaped clock calendar. When someone would ask Santa what day it was, he would reply, "It's half-past May," or "Quarter 'til November!" (RKC.)

THE CANDY CANE SIGNPOST. The park was located in Skyforest, in the San Bernardino mountains off Rim of the World Highway. Its concept, conceived by owner Glenn Holland, was that guests were visiting Santa's year-round home and workshop. Inspired by his friends, Dick and Mac McDonald and Ray Kroc of McDonald's fame, Holland opened two more Santa's Villages in Santa Cruz and Dundee, Illinois. Santa's Village was America's first amusement park franchise. (RKC.)

JACK-IN-THE-BOX SNACK BAR. Jack looms from his scented box as elves and children cuddle with and bottle-feed baby goats, which roamed Santa's Village along with other animals. Graceful swans could be found swimming in Silver Slipper Lake, near the Enchanted Castle. About 70 costumed gnomes worked at the village. A herd of 30 reindeer was imported from Alaska. (RKC.)

SANTA'S SPECIAL GUESTS. Since chimps were all the rage in the mid-20th century, naturally, Santa welcomed guests like these adorable twin baby chimpanzees. Southlanders enjoy reminiscing about events such as the annual pet parade along with the post office, where postcards could be sent with a "Santa's Village" postmark, Santa's Toy and Game House, and the Candy Kitchen, where visitors could watch taffy being pulled and sugar spun for lollipops and candy canes. (RKC.)

FAIRYLAND TRAIN RIDE. The train at Santa's Village was built by Hurlbut Amusement Co. and took passengers through the Lollipop Forest; the homes of Hansel and Gretel; Little Miss Muffet; Peter, Peter, Pumpkin Eater; and Santa's private goldmine. Other rides included a pumpkin carriage, the bumblebee monorail, and a roller coaster. When the park closed in 1998, the train was bought by the Santa Ana Zoo. (RKC.)

SPINNING ORNAMENTS RIDE. Christmas- and fantasy-themed rides made visits to Santa's Village all the more magical. From the 1950s to the 1990s, generations enjoyed the excursion to Skyforest; for some, it was an annual tradition before or after Christmas. Others did not mind visiting in August, when temperatures would climb above 90 degrees; photographs show visitors in shorts and tank tops. (RKC.)

LOLLIPOP LADY AND FRIENDS. J. Putnam Henck—the park's vice president and co-contractor—and his wife, Pamela (third from left), became owners of Santa's Village in 1978. A new cast of characters, like Pamela's Lollipop Lady and the guitar-strumming Rainbow Man, joined long-timers like the Easter Bunny and Jack Pumpkinhead. The park's closing in 1998 marked "the end of a certain age of innocence," Henck told the *Los Angeles Times*. In 2016, SkyPark at Santa's Village opened under the ownership of Michelle and Bill Johnson. (RKC.)

ENCHANTED FOREST FANTASY PLAYLAND, 1961.
Its theme was the Brothers Grimm's 14th-century
Black Forest, inhabited by witches, gnomes, and
other European storybook characters. There was
Whimsy Castle, cars pulled by deer, and Little
People costumed as elves. Children could fly in giant
hummingbirds while adults visited Genie's Magic
Candles. Somehow, kids did not love it, everyone
lost money, and, after it hosted the National Field
Archery Championships in 1963, its medieval gates
in Running Springs closed for good. (RKC.)

WILD RIVERS OF IRVINE. Upon the grounds where wild animals once roamed, a waterpark opened
in 1986. Lion Country Safari became Wild Rivers Waterpark. When temperatures got warm,
residents and tourists could not resist shooting down slides like the Congo River Rapids and
Bombay Blasters. For younger children, there was the Pygmy Pond, Typhoon Lagoon, and the
Dinosaur Slide. Next door was Irvine Meadows Amphitheatre, which hosted artists like Michael
Jackson and Bon Jovi. The waterpark closed in 2011.

LAKE DOLORES, MOJAVE DESERT. Boasting the West Coast's first and biggest high-speed waterslide, Lake Dolores was created by the Byers family in the 1960s. Located in Yermo, the park featured giant trapeze-like swings over a lake, Skeeter and bumper boats, a zip-cord cable for swinging across the water, go-carts, and a miniature golf course. After closing, the park became Rock-a-Hoola in 1998 and Discover Waterpark in 2002 before closing permanently in 2004.

Five

MIDCENTURY AMUSEMENT PARKS

Nowhere was Modernist design more prevalent after World War II than in Southern California. Many of the nation's top architects graduated from schools like the University of Southern California (USC), and leading talent gravitated toward the region, where there was capital, a need for commercial and residential buildings, and openness for exuberant, futurist design. With Disneyland in 1955, high-end amusement parks exploded in the Southland, bringing visitors and revenue that was unprecedented.

Before Disneyland, there was Marineland, which opened in 1954 in Rancho Palos Verdes on land offering breathtaking views of the Pacific and designed by the formidable architectural firm of William Pereira and Charles Luckman. "Marineland was something very new: an outdoor marine zoo combining entertainment and education," said Alan Hess, architect, author, and Midcentury Modern historian. "Pereira & Luckman's designs are excellent examples of International Style Modernism, expressing the muscular structures needed functionally to hold those big tanks of water and amphitheaters for seating."

In 1958, another seaside amusement park opened where Venice meets Santa Monica. Pacific Ocean Park (POP) was an imaginative land-and-sea venture designed by film studio scenic artists headed by Fred Harpman. "Pacific Ocean Park was heavily influenced by the pleasure piers built along the coast for decades, but which were becoming seedy," said Hess. "Its architecture repeated the rides and attractions people expected on piers, but they were given Modern styles for a new look."

A decade later, Anheuser-Busch brought tourists inland, commissioning architects Thornton Ladd and John Kelsey to design a park integrated with the company's Van Nuys brewery. "Busch Gardens was distinguished by its landscaping," said Hess. "Ladd & Kelsey were very well-respected Modern architects, and the quality of their architectural designs was quite sophisticated for a theme park and blended with the landscape and planning very well.

"All three parks were distinctly Modern, showing that Modern design was widely popular in postwar Southern California," said Hess. "They also were responses to the growing population's need and desire for recreation, a place to take the family. While their roots were in older recreation types (Coney Island, city parks), each was in its unique way a creative updating of those needs."

MARINELAND OF THE PACIFIC. Marineland of Rancho Palos Verdes was home to the biggest oceanarium in the world when it opened in 1954. William Pereira was a chief shaper of mid-20th-century California architectural design. Among his achievements were CBS Television City, the Disneyland Hotel, and the Los Angeles Zoo. Pereira and Charles Luckman also worked out Marineland's challenging engineering details. Architect Gin Wong contributed to the Marineland project as president of Pereira & Luckman. (GMA.)

THE SKY TOWER, 1966. Marineland executives Henry Harris and William Monahan stand beside the 244-foot-tall Sky Tower, which was a fascinating four-minute ride with views of the park and the Pacific. Marineland featured the world's largest saltwater tank. Both of its tanks were 30 feet high, with one measuring 80 feet across, and included a 1,500-seat grandstand around two-thirds of its perimeter. The 90-acre park's two exhibition tanks were built to hold sharks, manta rays, and whales. (UCLA.)

FIRST OF ITS KIND ON THE WEST COAST. Opening day festivities were held on August 28, 1954, and featured the US Coast Guard and Alice in Marineland, who tossed the first fish in the porpoise show. As the crowd watched, curator Kenneth Norris and his staff introduced the aquatic mammal cast to their new environment. Stars of the Oceanarium show included 200-pound porpoises, more than 100 sharks, and a 75-pound electric eel. (Craig Christensen.)

WINDOWS TO THE OCEAN FLOOR. Guests at Marineland could observe aquatic animals inside the tanks through 1,500 separate windows at three different levels. Fish on display included moray eels, stingrays, giant sea turtles, and porpoises. Resembling the central character of the 1960s TV series *Diver Dan*, deep-sea divers could be viewed feeding and interacting with fish. All had reportedly endured fish bites but would not let that stop them from doing their jobs. (GMA.)

AN INTERNATIONAL LEADER IN MARINE RESEARCH. By 1964, Marineland had built 12 saltwater tanks, populated by 65 sea mammals, 3,000 fish of 100 different species, and waterfowl from five continents. Still a marine amusement park, the oceanarium used its 10th anniversary to emphasize its recognition as an international center for scientific research of marine mammals and oceanography. Reportedly the first to catch whales alive on the open sea, Marineland's oceanographers and marine biologists researched training, feeding, and medical care of whales, dolphins, sea lions, walruses, and seals. (GMA.)

TRAINED MARINE MAMMALS. While it strived to present an educational experience, Marineland was also in the entertainment business. Occasionally, surprise celebrity guests like Jayne Mansfield or actors from television series like The Munsters joined the sea animals. These appearances were sometimes televised, helping to promote the park and the performers' own current projects. In 1962, Sea Hunt actor Lloyd Bridges met six Atlantic dolphins at Los Angeles International Airport (LAX) that relocated from Florida to join Marineland. (GMA.)

CELEBRITY SEA LIFE. Marineland's first resident was Miss Granda Cahuama, a 300-pound green sea turtle from Mexico. Others joined her from the waters off Southern California and Mexico. Locals who frequented the park might remember stars like porpoises Frankie and Floyd; Woofy the walrus; Elsie the Pacific dolphin; killer whales Corky, Orky, and Swifty; and Bubbles the whale. Some dolphins leaped through rings of fire, while Frankie and Floyd jumped out of the water to retrieve fish from the trainer's hand. (JC.)

THE GEDDINGS FAMILY, MARINELAND SIGN, C. 1958. Many Southlanders enjoyed taking Sunday drives to Palos Verdes, where they could cruise through the Hollywood Riviera from the north or Long Beach from the south. Located nearby were the Lloyd Wright–designed Wayfarer's Chapel and Point Vicente Lighthouse. In 1958, Marineland's larger Sea Arena was built with stadium seating for 3,000. Bubbles, a 13-foot, 1,600-pound black pilot whale, was the star attraction. (The Geddings family.)

OVERHEAD OF RESTAURANT COMPLEX. The circular Marineland Restaurant, Porpoise Room lounge, and Penguin Room were adjacent to the park. In 1969, the restaurant became Galley West. Marineland changed ownership and was known as Hanna-Barbera's Marineland in the late 1970s–early 1980s. In 1987, Harcourt Brace Jovanovich (owners of SeaWorld) bought it and moved all the animals to SeaWorld. A resort now sits on the property. (Keane Arase, Keane's Pics.)

PORPOISE ROOM AT MARINELAND RESTAURANT. This fabulous bar featured a giant faux shell soffit decorated with real shells and tiny lights. Also designed by Pereira & Luckman, this spectacular glass-enclosed circular dining complex offered unhindered views. Live music was featured nightly for the cocktail-dinner crowd, including name acts like the Ink Spots and the Matt Dennis Trio. Thousands of sparkling shells and rocks also adorned the outside entrance and lobby, accented by waterfalls and pools. (James Brouwer.)

PACIFIC OCEAN PARK. This fabulous sea-themed amusement park opened in part to compete with Disneyland. Spearheaded by CBS and the Los Angeles Turf Club, the park opened in 1958 on 28 acres of land and sea where Santa Monica meets Venice. Fred Harpman oversaw the talented amusement park designers, Hollywood scenic artists, and special effects wizards, creating what the Venice *Evening Vanguard* described as an "oceanic wonderland with sparkling, contemporary design." (Ernest Marquez Collection, the Huntington Library, San Marino, California.)

ENTRANCE, NEPTUNE'S COURTYARD. Pacific Ocean Park (POP) guests walked through the futuristic, now iconic Starfish Arch that supported giant seahorses and floating bubbles to enter a glittering courtyard with statuary, shimmering fountains, and waterfalls powered by Aquatechnics. Visitors took a giant undersea elevator leading to real and robotic fish swimming through coral and sea gardens. (JBH.)

UNION 76 OCEAN HIGHWAY. Children and adults drove miniature gas-powered cars on a quarter-mile track that traveled up, down, and around the park and above the Pacific. The ride was similar to Disneyland's Autopia. About 75 feet above the Ocean Highway was the Ocean Skyway, a tramway that transported bubble-shaped gondolas one-half mile across the park to the end of the pier and back. (BA.)

FLIGHT TO MARS. In ads (inset, upper right), this atomic-age, mostly walk-through attraction promised a trip to Mars. Inside, guests sat in the simulated flying saucer's circular room, viewing films of celestial objects on television monitors. The journey was possible through the high-tech magic of strobe, pinpoint, ultraviolet, and black lights; mirrors; blasts of air; static electricity; and sliding doors. Imaginative artwork and figures depicting otherworldly animals and plants indicated visitors truly were on Mars. (BA.)

MYSTERY ISLAND BANANA TRAIN RIDE. Trains entered a jungle teeming with rare, South Seas tropical plants and inhabited by wild animals and cannibals. During the trip, riders experienced an earthquake (very California), tropical storm, and found themselves amid an active volcano. In the tiki-themed South Seas Island section, Mystery Island was at the tip of the pier, with parts of the ride precariously hovering over the ocean. (BA.)

ENTRANCE TO THE SEA TUBS. With experienced, talented designers producing whimsical work, POP appears to have been a somewhat fantastical, slightly counterculture mash-up of Disneyland and Marineland. Some rides were daring, and others were standards disguised in oceanic themes and decor. A giant octopus with head and tentacles popping through the building's facade was the entrance for the Sea Tubs. Supposedly, the artist was inspired by Pres. Dwight Eisenhower when he sculpted the octopus's bulbous cranium. (BA.)

THE FLYING PARATROOPER. The park's 1959 expansion included the Paratrooper swing ride with flying saucer-like roofs. A lap bar made sure riders were safe, although this was the type of ride in which hysterical teens would clutch each other's arms. That year, other new rides were introduced: Twirly Bird helicopters, U-Drive-It boats, and the Haunted Tree Maze. (JBH.)

PEPE'S PIZZA. Designed as a giant basket-woven jug (of Chianti?), Pepe's was one of POP's most popular food concessions. Additional places to dine included the New England-style Fisherman's Cove area with fish 'n' chips and hamburgers. In the quieter International Promenade area around the corner were restaurants like the Steinhaus, Tzu Hat Pin, and the British Sea Horse Inn. (JBH.)

ENTRANCE TO THE CAROUSEL. The merry-go-round was housed in a building featuring slightly abstract sculptures of children on carousel-rocking horses. It was located along with other rides and concessions in POP's midway, which was called the more enticing Ports o' POP. Ocean Park Pier's former High Boy roller coaster was cleaned up and became the Sea Serpent. (JBH.)

BUMPY RIDE AHEAD. Everyone enjoyed bumper cars, which were called Sea Rams at POP. After a few years, the dazzling rides and attractions started to lose their sheen. Attendance dropped, Santa Monica wanted to redevelop the area, and POP went bankrupt. A decade after opening, a *Los Angeles Times* cover image showed two sad-looking kids on the carousel. "Without life and laughter," said a ride operator in the *Times*, "the amusement industry is deader than Pacific Ocean Park." (JBH.)

BUDWEISER PAVILION, BUSCH GARDENS. Opened in 1966, the $4 million project was a fusion of a theme park and a tropical oasis that spread across 17 acres adjacent to the Anheuser-Busch Brewery in Van Nuys. It was designed by the leading architectural firm of Thornton Ladd and John Kelsey, known for their designs of the Pasadena Art Museum (later the Norton Simon), CalArts University, and the Stuft Shirt in Newport Beach. (HBC.)

OPENING DAY, MAY 26, 1966. On hand for the ribbon-cutting and grand-opening festivities at the Skyrail were August A. Busch, Anheuser-Busch president and chairman of the board; Los Angeles mayor Sam Yorty; and the other chairman of the board, Frank Sinatra. Some 260 guests enjoyed lunch with the Busch family, brewery tours via monorails, walks in the lush gardens, and boat cruises through the tropical paradise. (UCLA.)

THE RIVERBOAT CRUISE. The park was plotted into three connecting sections: Palm Island, the Gorge, and the Central Lagoon. Boarding one of the 22-passenger riverboats gave visitors a chance to meander lagoons and lakes. Boat operators pointed out water-loving birds, including herons, swans, egrets, and flamingoes. More than 1,000 birds called Busch Gardens "home," and it became a popular place for photographers and ornithologists to get close-up images. (HBC.)

The Bavarian Pavilion. The three identical Bavarian Pavilions were built 22 feet above the water to offer stunning views. Busch Gardens' architecture and landscape were designed to blend with the subtropical temperatures of the San Fernando Valley. Continuing the original Busch Gardens' emphasis on landscaping (it was a park in Pasadena 1906–1937), Anheuser-Busch hired landscape architect /horticulturist Morgan "Bill" Evans to join Ladd & Kelsey in designing the property. Evans did part of the landscaping for Disneyland and Disney World. (HBC.)

The Scenic Gorge. Rock formations in the Gorge section of Busch Gardens were made of volcanic feather rock, which was brought from California's Mono Lake area. The Gorge featured dramatic, craggy heights and a thundering waterfall, scenes often depicted in beer ads to emphasize the fresh water used in its products. (HBC.)

THE MODERNIST MONORAIL. At the park's dedication, August Busch said, "It is our belief that a modern industrial plant can add to the area by design and landscaping." Actor/announcer Ed McMahon narrated the Skyrail tour, which allowed visitors to observe the brewing and packaging process. McMahon appeared in Budweiser ads, suggesting that consumers "Pick a Pair" of six-packs while shopping. Following a tour that snaked through buildings and the park, guests strategically debarked at a beer pavilion. (HBC.)

BUSCH GARDENS' MICHELOB TERRACE. For its first few years, beer was free, and the park provided areas for guests to enjoy their beer while admiring the view. In 1969, citizens formed a group to protest overflow parking in nearby neighborhoods. Apparently adding to the problem were drivers who left Busch Gardens "intoxicated by free beer," a woman complained to the *Los Angeles Times*. (HBC.)

BUSCH GARDENS ADDS MORE BIRDS. Visitors could walk through a series of interwoven paths, enjoying gardens filled with bamboo, palms, and tropical flowers. Flamingo Island (pictured) became part of the Lagoon section. More than 2,000 birds were added for shows, with stars like macaws, toucans, parrots, and macaws. Although they were relocated to other zoos, a legend perpetuates that exotic birds observed in the "wilds" of the San Fernando Valley are descendants of Busch Gardens birds. (HBC.)

YA-HOO FLUME RIDE. To compete with nearby amusement parks, Busch Gardens added more attractions and rides in the early 1970s. In 1975, part of the park became Old St. Louis, based on the 1904 World Exposition in St. Louis, Missouri, and the 1852 establishment of Anheuser-Busch in the same city. In 1977, the park became the Busch Bird Sanctuary; two years later, it closed. Anheuser-Busch felt an expansion of the brewery would be more profitable than a theme park. (HBC.)

Six

SEASIDE PARKS AND ATTRACTIONS

Southern California has a long history of pleasure piers and seaside attractions along its roughly 200-mile coastline. Railways and trolleys made them accessible to city dwellers. Blackouts and dimouts during World War II affected amusement parks, but the remaining few helped to entertain civilians and troops on leave during a turbulent time. Postwar, some parks with midways, tattoo parlors, girlie shows, and concessions took on an adults-only vibe, especially after dark. Even with classic rides still intact, many families avoided pier parks. What had once been the quintessential Southern California experience—an afternoon at the beach followed by a casual dinner and an evening cooling off on a Ferris wheel—became all but forgotten. Families moved to affordable housing in the suburbs, away from cities and the coast. Television and the rituals of everyday life took precedence over those spontaneous days and evenings at the beach.

Still, some hung in there. Mission Beach's Belmont Park stayed open for sailors and locals during the war but had its ups, downs, and rebirths, with a historic 1925 Giant Dipper wooden roller coaster and indoor saltwater pool, the Plunge, at the center of restoration efforts. The Long Beach Pike endured changes in ownership, jurisdiction, and names, along with fires and the devastating Long Beach Earthquake in 1933. In the early 1950s, a contest rebranded it the Nu-Pike, which sounded promising for a postwar world. Down the coast, the Balboa Fun Zone remains a shadow of its halcyon years during the mid-20th century. The permanent arcade that was the Fun Factory in Redondo Beach was all that remained of former rides and games on the pier, closing in 2019. In the early 1900s, Venice Beach boasted beautiful buildings and rides but became a victim of the Depression, Prohibition, and fires. Venice's seedy reputation persisted throughout and after the war. In 1950, Venice Lake Park opened for less than a year, followed by Hoppyland, which lasted a few years and mostly catered to children.

Ocean Park Pier evolved into Pacific Ocean Park in Santa Monica, which was history by 1968. Newer Southern California amusement parks were becoming upscale and technologically and artistically advanced. Owners realized the importance of cleanliness and safety. A casual day at a seaside park became yet another part of our collective past.

BALBOA FUN ZONE. This little bayfront amusement park in Newport Beach was a favorite for decades. Built in 1936, it entertained generations of beachgoers and tourists. Balboa Fun Zone endured closures and reopenings; in 1994, a former fun zone employee tried to resurrect it. In 2006, rides were removed for a nautical museum. Favorites like the carousel, a scary dark ride, miniature golf, and bumper cars were phased out; the small Ferris wheel and a few shops remain. (OCA.)

SPRING BREAK, "BAL WEEK." For decades, thousands of high school and college students (and some younger) would alight on Balboa Island for spring break. Nearby rentals were grabbed up in advance, and students would camp out in sleeping bags. They did not care; the seven days of fun, flirting, and hanging with friends were worth it. Bal Week started in the late 1920s and continued through the late 1960s, when police and landlords put an end to the nonstop parties. (UCIHM.)

FUN ZONE, OVERHEAD. Balboa Fun Zone featured a carousel, Ferris wheel, bumper cars, and other rides. Part of the fun was taking the ferry from Balboa Peninsula to Balboa Island. The ferry opened in 1919 and is still in operation. The late legendary surf guitarist Dick Dale had a record shop on the peninsula in the late 1950s–early 1960s. In the evenings, he and his band, the Del-Tones, would perform at the Rendezvous Ballroom. (OCA.)

COEDS AT GAME BOOTH. Bal Week crowds would visit the Fun Zone, swim, rent boats, sunbathe, and go to the Rendezvous at night. The club was a place to hear live bands, dance, and meet other young singles. "Once you were on the peninsula, you couldn't get off," said Dale in a 1990 interview with the *Los Angeles Times*. "Everybody had a party on every single front porch. There were about a hundred kids on everyone's porch." The Rendezvous burned in 1966. (UCIHM.)

BEACH AT THE FUN ZONE. Bal Week crowds were known to topple lifeguard towers, bury their friends in the sand, and dive off any high perch they could find. In the evening, it was time to clean up (there was a dress code) and hit the Rendezvous, where everyone was learning the surfer stomp to Dick Dale and the Del-Tones. (UCIHM.)

GAMES OF CHANCE. The Fun Zone's old-fashioned arcade and concessions were a novelty for some children who never visited pleasure piers or carnivals. Games included air rifles, basketball, darts, or Skee-Ball. Prizes were chalkware figurines or plush toys—the bigger, the better. Food was typical amusement park cuisine: cotton candy, hot dogs, soda, and Balboa bars and frozen bananas, for which Balboa is famous. (OCA.)

BALBOA BEAUTY CONTEST, C. 1946. The 1950s–1960s were probably the golden age for beauty pageants and contestants. Staging one at Balboa combined all the right ingredients: pretty girls, sunshine, swimsuits, and crowds who would spend money at the Fun Zone. Balboa beauty pageants date back at least to the 1920s, when they focused on "bathing beauties." (UCIWG.)

PIRATE DAYS AT BALBOA, 1953. Another annual celebration was Pirate Days, usually held in September over a three-day weekend. Participants donned their best pirate costumes. Those not dressed in pirate garb were thrown in a "real" pirate jail. The festivities included a parade, a celebration at the Fun Zone, and the crowning of a pirate king and queen. Other activities included tug-of-war, a street dance, and a beauty roundup (pictured). (UCIHM.)

THE LONG BEACH PIKE. Since 1902, the amusement park at Long Beach was one of Southern California's biggest and best. It endured ownership changes, fires, the 1933 Long Beach Earthquake, and economic hardships but was always there to entertain Southlanders after a day at the beach or a swim at its saltwater plunge. In the early 1950s, a contest was held to select a new name. The winner: Nu-Pike. (Unofficial US Navy Site.)

PONIES AND THE CYCLONE, c. 1954. Little Stevie Cardwell was all decked out in his finest cowboy outfit when he rode a pony at the Nu-Pike, against the backdrop of the magnificent Cyclone Racer, a wooden, dual-track roller coaster that made twists and turns over the ocean. The Cyclone was built in 1930 and dismantled in 1969. Advertisements boasted the Nu-Pike had "Eight Big Blocks of Fun." (Glenn S. Cardwell.)

THE WILD MAUS. Introduced around 1960, this wooden roller coaster operated until 1979. Nu-Pike became Queen's Park in the late 1960s to coincide with the arrival of the *Queen Mary.* "The drops are really exhilarating," wrote William Jones in 1961 in the Long Beach *Press-Telegram.* "Air is forced into your lungs. The moistness of the fog makes your face get really wet." Cyclone's drops were 60 miles per hour, with "bone-wracking turns." (NDF.)

SKY WHEEL DOUBLE FERRIS WHEEL. Nu-Pike's Sky Wheel was manufactured by Chance Amusements and the Allan Herschell Company, Inc. A Sky Wheel had 16 seats, which accommodated about 32 people. The experience was one of rapidly being propelled into the sky, then going into a free fall as the wheels rotate downward. (NDF.)

ROTOR AFTER DARK. Rotor was a spinning drum that, when it reached maximum speed, the floor dropped, leaving riders plastered to the wall of the drum. Part of the attraction's entertainment was for those on the ground who enjoyed watching the reactions of their foolhardy friends and strangers. (NDF.)

MARFLEET'S FAMOUS HAMBURGERS. Located at 240 W. Pike, Arthur Marfleet sold hamburgers, hot dogs, chili, and beef stew for 37 years to hungry customers. "I don't think any place is better known than we are," said Marfleet in a 1959 interview with the Long Beach *Independent*. "The Navy boys, of course, have carried the word of us around the globe." (John B. Mellquist.)

PARKING LOT, NU-PIKE, JUNE 1956. Melvina and Arthur Morning posed for a picture in the parking lot of Long Beach's Nu-Pike while some polite teenagers decided not to run in front of the camera. The Cyclone Racer can be seen in the distance. Judging by the cars in the lot, it seemed to be a good day to drive a Pontiac. Until 1961, people without cars could take the Pacific Electric rail line from Los Angeles to Long Beach. (The Morning/Winant families.)

PIKE SHOOTING GALLERY. Marion Kathy Symonds's first job was at the Pike arcade. The amusement park is where she met her husband, Lee George, whose uncle owned a club. Concessions were owned by an individual or families, many of whom took shifts to keep the business running morning through late in the evening. (The George family.)

105

LONG BEACH ARCADE JAIL. Pleasure piers bring out the playful side in some people, and the Sea Side Studio gave them a chance to goof off for the camera. A favorite photo opportunity at the Pike was a faux Long Beach Jail. A Los Angeles man and his daughters hammed it up with cigarettes dangling from their mouths as they did about five minutes in the slammer around 1950. Pictured from left to right are patriarch Anderson Franklin, Inez, Nellie (with hand over rail), Joan (directly behind Nellie), and Margaret. (The Franklin family.)

SNAKE CHARMER. At the Pike in the 1950s, Helen May Lay (right) worked the midway as a snake charmer, a headless woman, knife-throwing assistant, and the electric lady. The Pike had many colorful activities: there were coin-op peep shows, tattoo parlors, bars, restaurants, and nightclubs. Some loved the nightlife and action, while others felt it had become a gimcrack honky-tonk with hillbilly music and too many booze emporiums. (The Davis-Lay family.)

LAFF IN THE DARK. This dark ride had an even darker side that was not uncovered until 1976. A television crew member filming inside the ride accidentally dislodged an arm from a wax dummy, revealing the arm was bone. The story made headlines and alerted an Oklahoma museum staff, who believed the corpse was that of outlaw Elmer McCurdy, wanted for murder in 1911. At some point, McCurdy's (dead) body was sold to a traveling carnival. Elmer McCurdy was returned to Oklahoma for a proper burial.

VIRGINIA PARK GAYWAY, LONG BEACH. This amusement area next to the Nu-Pike entertained children not yet ready for the Cyclone and operated from about 1947 to 1958. A 1956 newspaper ad claimed that the Nu-Pike and Virginia Park were the "largest amusement park on the West Coast," the parks had a "Mammoth New Sea Lion Lagoon," and promised, "You'll find 1,000 new thrills." Beverly Park owner Dave Bradley managed Virginia Park for several years. (OCA.)

"THE PLACE WHERE FUN WAS INVENTED." In 1954, the sprawling seaside park was one of the top-five amusement centers in the nation and a favorite of Stevie Cardwell (pictured) and his family. With the studios nearby, the park was a popular filming location for movies, including *Roustabout* and *It's a Mad, Mad, Mad, Mad World*. In the 1970s, it continued to decline as Queen's Park, closing in 1979. In 2003, an entertainment complex, the Pike at Rainbow Harbor, opened. (Glenn S. Cardwell.)

ENTERING OCEAN PARK. After the war, the once-thriving Ocean Park Amusement Pier was renovated. In a June 1949 newspaper ad, 14 rides were announced, including a roller coaster, Auto Skooter, Sky Chief, Sky Rider, Loop-O-Plane, Stratoliner, Diving Bell, Toonerville, and a Tilt-a-Whirl. (GMA.)

CIRCUS GARDENS, OCEAN PARK PIER. Formerly the Casino Gardens, Circus Gardens opened in 1953 with a five-hour show featuring circus acts, ice performers, ballet and can-can dancers, and burlesque stars. Located at Ocean Park's Fun Zone, the Circus Garden sign was a perfect backdrop for the many beauty, swimsuit, and bodybuilding contests staged at nearby Venice and Santa Monica beaches. (GMA.)

TOONERVILLE AT OCEAN PARK. Toonerville Fun House was based on the *Toonerville Folks* comic strip of Fontaine Fox, about a ramshackle town with a rickety trolley and folksy citizens. The syndicated comic ran in more than 300 newspapers from the 1920s–1955. The attraction dated back to 1925, when the original Ocean Park Pier opened. Parts of Ocean Park Amusement Pier were razed after it closed in 1956. In the summer of 1958, it reopened as Pacific Ocean Park. (GMA.)

FINAL YEARS AT OCEAN PARK PIER. The pleasure pier was still popular in the 1950s. By 1958, the area was considered blighted and sought national funding for redevelopment. Other buildings were razed in the area to make way for high-rise apartments. In 1996, Pacific Park opened on Santa Monica Pier and has about 12 rides. (GM.)

REDONDO SKY LIFT. The little-known sky ride at the Redondo Beach Pier operated from 1965 to about 1967. Apparently, it was part of a Fisherman's Wharf expansion that was to include more rides and attractions. In 1972, the Sea Inn at the pier morphed into the Fun Factory, a bar with arcade games and rides. Locals loved Fun Factory's vibrance, vintage neon, and coin-op rides. Fun Factory closed in October 2019. (The LeFleur family.)

Seven

LOST RIDES AND ATTRACTIONS

The story of post–World War II amusement parks in Southern California is one of success for a handful that were built, established identities, appealed to many, and managed to revamp and reinvent when necessary. All made mistakes and learned from their own and one another's. What they have in common is survival.

Who would know now that Frontierland was Disneyland's most popular section when the park opened in July 1955? But Westerns and cowboys reigned supreme. Knott's already had an Old West theme with its Ghost Town and was in the process of expanding it when Disneyland opened. Westerns were touched upon with a train ride when Magic Mountain opened in 1971, but by then, children were into other things. SeaWorld started with a very defined theme—the ocean and marine animals—and Universal Studios' focus was on television and movie making.

To cover all of the rides that have come and gone at existing parks is inconceivable, as there are hundreds. Some were much loved, like Knott's Bear-y Tales, which was recently brought back in a new ride that pays tribute to the first one from the 1970s. Other attractions had short lives. Does anyone remember Frontierland's Mineral Hall?

That rides do survive is a testament to their original concepts; some were brilliant, able to transcend time, used unprecedented technology, were visually beautiful, or had something else that cannot be explained. Who could have predicted that the birds of the Enchanted Tiki Room would still be enthralling audiences decades later? Or that the thrill of going down that last drop on Knott's log ride still elicits screams of delight, with or without a candid souvenir photograph?

Imagine what an amusement park ride goes through, day after day, even with a maintenance crew to keep it in top shape? Rides at full-time parks have a structural wear-out at about the 15-year mark, explained Robin Stewart Hall, who headed up the design departments for Magic Mountain and Knott's Berry Farm and has worked on amusement park planning and ride designs for parks throughout the world. "While you may see a coaster or a flume at a park for a longer time (than 15 years), it has been rebuilt with new parts nearly from start to finish," explained Hall. "The longer the ride is in place, the greater the cost it is to maintain."

SeaWorld of Mission Bay. The park opened on 21 acres in 1964 and was founded by four graduates of the University of California, Los Angeles, whose original idea of an underwater restaurant/aquatic theater was not approved. One, George Millay, had restaurant experience as owner of the upscale tiki restaurants Ports O' Call in San Pedro and the Reef in Long Beach.

Theatre of the Sea. One of the early attractions included the Theatre of the Sea, which could accommodate 900 spectators peering through its 20-foot glass windows. A three-act drama featured a cast starring dolphins, sea maidens, and a hero. Victor Gruen Associates designed SeaWorld's master plan in 1960. *Los Angeles Times* columnist Art Seidenbaum called SeaWorld's architecture and landscaping "Honolulu Modern."

STARKIST UNDERWATER THEATRE. Narrated by Sebastian Cabot and with music by Nelson Riddle, this aquatic ballet included sea maidens, a seal named Max, and Humpty Dumpty. Another attraction, the Sparkletts Water Fantasy Show, featured a dazzling, changing display of water and colored lights synced to another Riddle score.

HYDROFOIL BOATS, MISSION BAY. SeaWorld's Richfield (later ARCO) Hydrofoil boats carried 28 passengers and clipped through Mission Bay. A 1971 ad described the experience: "You start out in the water and end up in the air. Riding on wings that skim the surface. Flying at 35 miles per hour."

SHAMU, THE KILLER WHALE. SeaWorld went through several whales they called Shamu and even trademarked the name. The whale became such a hit that Shamu Stadium was added in the early 1970s. Aquatic animals increased in popularity, and shows and performers were added. Among them were Google the Great, the "world's only trained elephant seal"; and penguins named John, Paul, George, and Ringo. (NDF.)

UNIVERSAL STUDIOS, 1969. The original tour opened in 1915 but closed with the advent of "talkies." Its 1964 reopening featured candy-striped GlamorTrams that provided behind-the-scenes looks at how movies were made, with an emphasis on special effects, props, wardrobe, and makeup. In the tour's early days, there was always the possibility of catching a television series or movies being filmed from a distance. (UCLA.)

114

STUNT PERFORMERS, UNIVERSAL, 1980. In the park's early years, arena shows demonstrated Hollywood stunts and pet training and tricks. When it opened in 1964, Westerns were still popular, and parts of *The Virginian* were shot on the lot. The tour also took visitors to the Glamour Pavilion, the Munster Laboratory, the Special Effects Set, and Photo Illusion Park, with oversized props. (Robert Ciavarro.)

MAGIC MOUNTAIN, VALENCIA. SeaWorld executive George Millay helped Magic Mountain become a reality in the master-planned community of Valencia. The park opened in 1971 and offered a variety of rides. Among them were the Gold Rusher roller coaster, the Log Jammer flume ride, El Bumpo bumper boats, and numerous kiddie rides, like this muscle car carousel. (RWH.)

ENTRANCE TO THE REVOLUTION. One of the first graduates of the California Institute of the Arts (CalArts), Robin Stewart Hall worked as Magic Mountain's art director and was chairman of the architectural committee for the Newhall Land and Farming Company, which is responsible for master planning the community of Valencia. The nation's bicentennial was a big event for amusement parks, and Magic Mountain's Revolution roller coaster paid tribute. (RSH.)

GRAND CENTENNIAL EXCURSION RAILROAD. Hall (left) and Douglas Booth (right) look over the construction of the railroad at Magic Mountain, which opened in 1975 and closed in 1985. The steam train took passengers through an Old West town and around the park's perimeter. During the mid-1970s, more rides debuted, like Magic Pagoda, Jolly Monster, Dragon, Mountain Express roller coaster, and Sierra Twist bobsleds. (RSH.)

COLOSSUS AT MAGIC MOUNTAIN. This much-anticipated and talked-about ride was the "world's tallest" and one of the fastest wooden roller coasters when it premiered in June 1978. It closed a year later for changes (reprofiling) around the same time that Six Flags bought the park. Colossus starred in the 1983 movie *National Lampoon's Vacation* as the coaster at Walley World. (UCLA.)

KNOTT'S RESIDENT CHARACTERS. Ghost Town's residents were a memorable bunch of Old West characters who roamed Main Street, chatted up tourists, and obligingly posed for photographs. Characters included Chief Red Feather; Deputy "Dude" Sands; Bud, the square dance caller; Higdon, the covered wagon driver; Sheriff Lewis; and Gus, the mule driver. Nathan Krotinger (right) hangs out with Arthur "Slim" Vaughn (left), the village Romeo. (The Krotinger family.)

KNOTT'S ADDS RIDES. In 1952, Knott's Berry Farm opened the Calico Railway. Sensing competition from what was to become Disneyland, patriarch Walter Knott enlisted family friend Wendell "Bud" Hurlbut, of Hurlbut Amusement Company, to suggest some rides. Knott bought Hurlbut's Dentzel carousel, and a business partnership was born. Hurlbut helped transform Knott's into a full-fledged amusement park, with rides like the Calico Mine Ride and Timber Mountain Log Ride. (OCA.)

SELF-PROPELLED SWING. 1955. Early rides at Knott's were not on par with their current high-tech marvels. The three Hermann brothers put forth a team effort to get this swing carousel to rotate, or at least budge. In 1957, Knott's added Henry's Livery, a car track for gas-powered miniature automobiles, each equipped with two steering wheels. (RH.)

INTERACTING WITH ANIMALS. Many Southland children and tourists had pictures taken with the monkey and the organ grinder at Knott's. Fearless Joel Weber (foreground) crawled on the ground and got the monkey to jump on his back. (Also pictured are Wilma Weber, in cat-eye sunglasses, with young Julia Weber, left, and George Otto Jr., right). Locals recall the touch of the monkey's tiny fingers as it snatched coins, put them in its pocket, and tipped its hat. (The Weber family.)

KNOTT'S BEAR-Y TALES, 1975. This is one example in which a ride was so missed, it came back again. The original and much beloved dark ride at Knott's was designed by Rolly Crump and was a whimsical sensory experience with friendly bears and frogs, a catchy theme song, and the aroma of boysenberries throughout (a Crump touch). Knott's Bear-y Tales: Return to the Fair opened in May 2021. (OCA.)

KINGDOM OF THE DINOSAURS. Hall was vice president of design and architecture at Knott's Berry Farm for 17 years. He and his team were given about six months to replace Knott's Bear-y Tales with Kingdom of the Dinosaurs. Using the same Bear-y Tales tracks, a new dark ride was created in which passengers entered a prehistoric land with 23 hissing, snapping, roaring, and chomping dinosaurs. (RSH.)

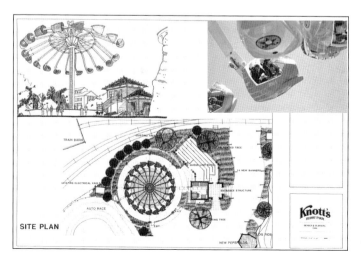

FLIGHT TRAINER, XK-1. Part of Knott's Boardwalk section, the XK-1 thrill ride was a Hall design that opened in 1989. Guests boarded capsules that circled a tower about 70 feet above ground and pivoted upside down. XK-1 was modified two years later so riders could no longer turn upside down. It was closed in 1997 and replaced by Supreme Scream. (Concept drawing, RSH; inset, OCA.)

THE FIRST AUTOPIA RACERS. When Autopia opened at Disneyland in July 1955, four of its 40 gas-powered cars were black-and-white police cars, complete with flashing red lights. Walt Disney had his own custom car, a metallic maroon with upholstery made of red nylon boucle and off-white leatherette. It was called the Disneyland Autopia Special, reported the *Long Beach Press-Telegram*. (OCA.)

NIXON WITH SPACE PEOPLE. Orange County native and vice president Richard M. Nixon visited Disneyland one month after its July 1955 opening to ceremoniously cut the ribbon for the monorail and treat his family to a fun trip to the world's most-talked-about amusement park. While there, he likely discussed the future with Spaceman X-7 and Spacegirl. (UCLA.)

MONSANTO HOUSE. When it opened in 1957, the *Los Angeles Times* described it as "a forerunner of the dwelling the typical American family of four may be living in 10 years from now." During the preview, a giant key to the future was presented to Wendy Stuart, 11, the Housewife of the Future. The plastic house was equipped with microwave cooking, ultrasonic dishwashing, and push-button telephones. After touring the home, Stuart closed her eyes and said, "I must be dreaming!" (Steve Fasnacht.)

TOMORROWLAND ASTRO JETS. This was considered a long line when the Astro Jets opened at Disneyland in 1956. Located between Flight (or Rocket) to the Moon and the Submarine Voyage, this spinning rocket ride was renamed the Tomorrowland Jets in 1964 and the Rocket Jets in 1967 when it was relocated and basically rebuilt during the Tomorrowland remodel. (The Connors family.)

Space Station Flying Saucers. Located near the Rocket to the Moon, the saucers debuted in 1961 and accommodated one or two people. Riders climbed aboard, fastened their seatbelts, and took off in free flight, with the sensation of hovering a few inches above ground, on a cushion of air. A sweeping broom-like device gathered them all together at the end of the ride. The ride closed in 1966. (The Connors family.)

Goodyear's PeopleMover. Debuting in 1967, PeopleMover was the transportation system of the future and considered as a prototype for intercity public transport. PeopleMover was removed in 1995. (UCLA.)

COMING ATTRACTIONS BOARD. A map with descriptions of upcoming plans was a smart way to make sure guests returned soon. In June 1959, the future looked bright, with the upcoming Submarine Voyage, an Autopia update, a Motor Boat Cruise, and the Glacier Grotto. In an August 1959 *Los Angeles Times* ad, Disneyland thanked the typical visitor for making tourism in Orange County its top industry. (Steve Fasnacht.)

THE ARCADE, A LOOK INTO THE PAST. Not everything was futuristic at midcentury Disneyland. Children seemed to be fascinated with the coin-operated machines found in the arcade, with about 130 antique machines to entertain them. The Mutoscopes these children were peering into were either hand-cranked or were electric Cail-o-scopes. (NDF.)

FUTURISTIC WORLD CLOCK. When Tomorrowland opened in 1955, it transported visitors to 1986, "where our hopes and dreams for the future become today's reality," reported a Disneyland supplement in the *Los Angeles Times*. "At a glance, this elaborate chronometer tells you the exact minute and hour anywhere on the face of the planet Earth." Trans World Airlines' Rocket to the Moon can be seen behind the World Clock. (RH.)

IT'S A GREAT BIG BEAUTIFUL TOMORROW. In July 1967, six months after the death of Walt Disney, Mickey Mouse hosted the premiere of its updated Tomorrowland. In keeping with corporation-sponsored rides and attractions, Disneyland 1967's futuristic offerings included General Electric's

Carousel of Progress; Monsanto's Adventure Through Inner Space; the self-piloting thrill ride, Rocket Jets; and the groovy Tomorrowland Terrace, a 17,300-square-foot entertainment space with twinkling lights. (OCA.)

DISCOVER THOUSANDS OF LOCAL HISTORY BOOKS FEATURING MILLIONS OF VINTAGE IMAGES

Arcadia Publishing, the leading local history publisher in the United States, is committed to making history accessible and meaningful through publishing books that celebrate and preserve the heritage of America's people and places.

Find more books like this at
www.arcadiapublishing.com

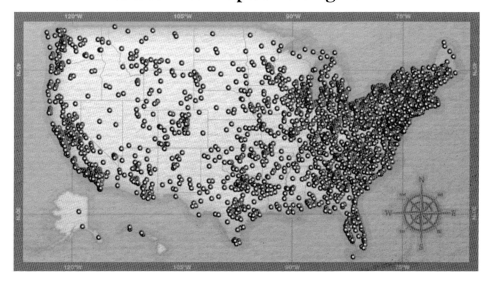

Search for your hometown history, your old stomping grounds, and even your favorite sports team.

Consistent with our mission to preserve history on a local level, this book was printed in South Carolina on American-made paper and manufactured entirely in the United States. Products carrying the accredited Forest Stewardship Council (FSC) label are printed on 100 percent FSC-certified paper.

MADE IN THE